The Sociology of Educational Ideas

The Sociology
of Educational Ideas

Julia Evetts

Department of Sociology
University of Nottingham

Routledge & Kegan Paul
London and Boston

First published in 1973
by Routledge & Kegan Paul Ltd,
Broadway House, 68-74 Carter Lane,
London EC4V 5EL and
9 Park Street,
Boston, Mass. 02108, USA
Printed in Great Britain by
Richard Clay (The Chaucer Press) Ltd,
Bungay, Suffolk
ISBN 0 7100 7609 6(c)
      0 7100 7619 3(p)
Library of Congress Catalog Card No. 72-97946

Editors' introductions

The Students Library of Education has been designed to meet the needs of students of Education at Colleges of Education and at University Institutes and Departments. It will also be valuable for practising teachers and educationists. The series takes full account of the latest developments in teacher-training and of new methods and approaches in education. Separate volumes will provide authoritative and up-to-date accounts of the topics within the major fields of sociology, philosophy and history of education, educational psychology, and method. Care has been taken that specialist topics are treated lucidly and usefully for the non-specialist reader. Altogether, the Students Library of Education will provide a comprehensive introduction and guide to anyone concerned with the study of education, and with educational theory and practice.

J. W. TIBBLE

The approach to educational ideas in this book reflects the way in which the scope of studies in the sociology of education has broadened during the past decade. From an early concern with the structural relationships of education and society, with problems of educational opportunity and the articulation of schooling and the labour market, sociologists have gone on to examine how knowledge is organised and managed, and the way in which our theories and ideas about man and society interact with our educational practices and procedures. Mrs Evetts takes a number of key concepts in education, such as those of intelligence, the educated man, equality of opportunity, the pool of ability, and compensatory education, and explores their social foundations and significance. She suggests that greater order can be introduced into the battle of 'warring parties, conflicting doctrines and alternative models' by relating the claims and counter claims of the participants to certain basic value assumptions. Mrs Evetts' book is a valuable counterpoise to the plethora of ideological statements about education that have attracted so much attention recently. It deserves to be read by all those students and teachers who are trying to find their way through the maze of educational ideas that are encountered today in university and college of education courses, and in the media.

WILLIAM TAYLOR

Contents

Introduction

In recent years, the sociology of education has centred around a number of important themes: social mobility, equality of opportunity, parity of esteem, IQ testing, the inadequacies of selection and streaming, the errors of a restrictionist interpretation of the reserves of ability and the class composition of the student body at grammar schools and universities. Such matters have been discussed and debated, and attempts have been made to make arguments precise and conclusive by the quantification of what are essentially qualitative concepts and the presentation of statistical evidence.

But far from clarifying the issues, this has resulted in a great deal of confusion, since many different and frequently contrasting interpretations have been made and conclusions drawn. How, for example, can Robin Pedley claim that comprehensive schools have GCE results which easily outstrip those of secondary schools in the maintained system as a whole (Tucker in Jackson and McAlhone, 1969), when R. R. Pedley (Cox and Dyson, 1969) quotes figures to show that in terms of A level passes, comprehensive schools did less well than grammar schools and, in fact, less well than the national average? What about Daniels' assertion (Jackson and McAlhone, 1969) that GCE examination results are not an appropriate criterion for comparing comprehensive and tripartite secondary schools? Professor Cyril Burt shows in *Black Paper* II that pupil attainment in basic skills has declined in our schools since 1913-14, yet Daniels presents statistics in *Verdict on the Facts* to show how standards have improved. Arthur Pollard's assertion (*Black Paper* II) that 'more means worse' is refuted by the editors (David Rubinstein and Colin Stoneman) of *Education for Democracy*.

Such examples could be multiplied. But dispute is not limited to the manipulation of statistics. Musgrave (1970) gives many examples of contrary generalisations being drawn from the same piece of historical evidence. Thus, while one author sees the Victorian public schoolboy drilled by his education into unthinking conformity, another sees in the same educational experience an ethic of 'frontier' independence which encouraged initiative. Disputes exist over every aspect of educational philosophy and practice, from pedagogy and selection in primary education to elitism and aimlessness in higher education. Assertions and counter-assertions of over-generalisation, of selectivity or of deliberate manipulation of statistics have become commonplace. We are familiar also with charges of inconsistency, bias and emotional outpourings, and of how truisms and inflated half-truths have led to exaggerated claims.

It is necessary to be aware from the start that one consequence of attempts to establish a science of things social, has been a strenuous drawing of the distinction between fact and value. A further consequence has been a collective blindness to the ways in which values themselves determine what one sees as facts. Another has been a tendency to accept that any factual study of social phenomena is its own justification. However, such consequences are untenable in education for it soon becomes obvious that, without values, no fact is more significant than any other. But values distort. They lead us to ignore certain causal chains, especially those which conflict with our own preconceptions, and to make more of other causal characteristics than the evidence alone would imply.

But it is even more important to recognise the interrelationship that exists between the different 'levels' of the education system and between education and the wider society. Sociologists concerned with education have paid too much attention to the demands of their audience or public, the teachers or potential teachers who, it was thought, needed some sociology of education to complete their already fragmented course. (In colleges of education and university departments of education, the courses usually consist of some combination between the philosophy of education, the psychology of the child, the sociology of education and the history of education.)

As a result, as a subject for study, the sociology of education has been divided up as follows: education as an institution and the relationship between education and other institutions in society (the family, social class, religion etc.); the school as an organisation, formal and informal structures; and the sociology of the classroom, the formation of groups and the interaction of pupils and teacher and pupils and pupils. These different levels of analysis have remained separate and distinct entities and any connections between them were purely incidental.

It is high time that sociologists interested in education began talking to their fellow sociologists. The interrelationship between educational ideas and educational structures needs to be understood. Formal education, like tradition, generally tends to be dependent upon particular forms of social organisation. The changes in educational outlook parallel the changes which a nation undergoes in the course of its history. The unifying factor in education reflects the dominance in each case of a given social body, e.g. church, class, nation. Education could be described as the manner by which these social bodies perpetuate themselves from generation to generation. Hence, education becomes transformed when there are social revolutions. Any attempt at social innovation includes consideration of educational methods and techniques. Because of this, considerations of the significance and methods of education inevitably include the larger question of state and society. Blueprints for the good society such as Plato's *Republic* treat political and educational organisation as coextensive. Education prepares each individual to be a member of society or, conversely, society is the means of the individual's education.

The social need of the times determines what will be included in the curriculum. Theological knowledge is required in preparation for the ministry; training in the skills of using language, for a humanistic education. For the education of the Greek gentleman a knowledge of myth and legend was required. Today, the importance of sociology, economics, technology, natural science and geography is stressed. Education changes with cultural ideals. The way schools are organised mirrors the social structure. In the past, diverse types of educational systems have been attempted such as schools for the several estates, academies for the nobility and private instruction for aristocrats and patricians. All democracies demand common public education because nothing makes people so much alike as the same education.

The question, what are the aims of education, continually asserts itself. Educational slogans do not amount to much. Defining ideals is a hopeless undertaking if we seek such ideals in a manner that ignores the actual historical situation and our own aims. In any case, ideals cannot be completely realised. There are two reasons for this. Opinions change as to which personal values are the most important ones. Various talents become more or less useful according to the sociological, economic and technical world situation. Moreover, every difference of competence is quickly frozen into formal status; for without stability and continuity, life could not go on. Thus, the ideal itself is exposed to corruption.

But it is necessary to start with our ideals. It is important that

3

we clarify the educational ideals and values that are behind certain existing structures and recommendations regarding those structures. It is important to realise that the same form of words may cloak different conceptions concerning the aims of education and very varied practical notions about what ought to be done. What we have to understand is not so much the form of words as the values implicit in the concrete and practical recommendations which the implementation of such views would necessitate. This is tackled in Part 1. Educational ideals are analysed by examining a number of key concepts in the education process such as intelligence, equal opportunity, knowledge and selection. It becomes clear that different and often contrasting interpretations of these concepts contain, implicitly or explicitly, sets of cognitive and moral assumptions about the nature of man, the genesis of knowledge, about the education process and its relationship to society. If we can isolate the definitions of the child and of education that compete for domination at any point in time, then we have a starting point for analysis of the main influences on the education system and of the processes at work within it. By examining two contrasting interpretations of education, a number of dilemmas emerge. These dilemmas amount to alternatives or choices as to how we regard the intellectual nature of man, the traditions of scholarship, the purpose of education and the relationship between education and society.

In Part II, this relationship between education and society is developed and examined, again by posing a number of dilemmas or choices as to how we are to regard the relationship. The implications of conceiving of education as a consumer item or as a social service are examined. Then we look at the idea that education and knowledge are 'managed' in order to further the achievement of some end or ideal society and see what the alternatives are in this respect. We next investigate the contention that it is important to examine the functions of the 'system' of education, and the opposing contention that the system's functions are meaningless and that we should concentrate instead on individual teachers' and pupils' perceptions of their aims and motives in education. Finally, in the last chapter, an attempt is made to assess the importance of educational ideals in policy and practice. When faced with a number of dilemmas, who is likely to opt for one alternative and who for another? Who has the power to make any alternative effective in terms of appropriate educational structures and organisations? How do these alternatives affect the processes at work within the organisations that are established?

Thus, by making explicit the principles that lie behind the dilemmas of education, important considerations about how things

4

are and about the sort of decisions that have to be faced in dealing with them, are clarified. We are better placed to understand the difficulties of explanation, justification and practical action in our educational system.

Part One

Exploring ideas in education

It is a sad feature of the current educational scene that attitudes and methods become polarised. The embattled paper tigers, empanoplied in red and black, raise their banners, chant their slogans and go to silly war.

T. R. Weaver, in a paper from the Department of Education and Science, 'Unity and Diversity in Education' (1970).

I

Contrasting approaches to education: 'progressives' and 'idealists' distinguished

To 'educate' people suggests a wide variety of 'aims' or 'goals', but a factor common to all of them is the idea of developing desirable qualities in the people concerned. However, there is no general consensus about which desirable qualities it should be the purpose of education to foster. Discussions concerning the aims of education are attempts, primarily, to specify more precisely what qualities it is thought desirable for education to develop. Any list of desirable qualities is not endless, however. There is some limit to what might count as an 'educational' end, since the concept of education also involves the development of knowledge and understanding. It is also implied that this understanding should not be too narrowly specialised (Hirst and Peters, 1970).

Throughout history, educationalists have debated what are necessary characteristics of the educated man. Obviously, opinions have differed; at different times and in different societies, certain qualities have been emphasised and others neglected. As opinions regarding the end product have differed, so also have opinions varied as to the most appropriate methods and contents to employ to achieve those ends.

In this country, today, it is possible to identify two distinct and contrasting approaches to education. Obviously this is to over-simplify the vast complexity of educational opinion and to do less than justice to the points of view involved, but it is a necessary and helpful simplification for the purpose of the analysis. The first approach will be called 'idealist'. The idealist educationalist may think that his purpose is to equip children with essential skills such as reading, spelling and arithmetic and to ensure that children are acquainted with necessary information. He may consider also that it is important to discipline children in certain sophisticated intellectual achievements, to mould their characters to a desirable shape and to instil respect for learning and scholarship. In this

9

case, children are taught to be adult and to respect and adopt adult values and goals. With such a purpose in mind, teaching methods will aim to encourage identification by children with educated men; by such means as competition and ranking, achievement goals are accepted. Children are formally instructed as a class and control is achieved by punishment, by competition and by stigmatising non-achievement. It is implicit in such a view that most children, if left undisturbed, cannot be expected to display much interest in academic pursuits that are outside their range of natural interests and understanding. Such an 'idealist' conception of education requires that education remain a stalwart of culture, quality and excellence; scholarship and learning should command the highest respect. Idealists see the main function of education as the passing on to each new generation of the best of the established and growing culture of their fathers. Such an interpretation of the 'educated man' contains implicit assumptions as to the nature of man and of society, and of the nature of knowledge and its genesis. Education is character-training; in the past this was the 'Christian gentleman' ideal; today this has been replaced by the detached, self-disciplined, rigorous scholar.

A contrasting view is more consistent with the assumption that 'education' is derived from the Latin 'educere' meaning 'to lead out'. Such a view believes the main function of education to be the training of the young for the new culture of the future. The aim of education is 'growth' or the development of individual potentialities. This second approach will be called 'progressive'. Progressives stress that teaching must be child-centred rather than subject-centred. The progressives' idea on teaching method can be related back to Pestalozzi, Dewey and Rousseau, with the curriculum based on the needs and interests of children. The child's own motivation and interest will determine the importance and significance of what is taught, since education is seen to be a 'drawing out' of each child's potential, of what each child has to offer. The aim of education is to enlarge the individual's capacity for experience by increasing the opportunities for him to learn through experience. Thus, methods are only educative if they involve learning from experience rather than the child being told things, and if the child discovers rather than merely listens.

'Education for life', 'child-centred education', 'the integrated curriculum' are all progressive aims just as 'academic excellence' and the 'maintenance of standards' are idealist aims. Do the terms progressive or idealist describe anything at all? Theoretically there are so many possible lines of educational thought that it seems meaningless to describe any one set of ideas as 'progressive' or 'idealist', for this would simply mean that supporters consider their ideas better than others, which is self-evident. However, the distinction does serve to separate the core elements of a number of distinct points of view. In practice, each does refer to a rather specific interpretation of the concept of 'education', and each contains a related body of educational ideas which are sufficiently distinct for the terms to be applied, even though the boundaries are not clearly defined. It is intended to show that, in the interpretation of key concepts in education such as 'intelligence' and 'knowledge', and in the assumed desirable relationship between education and society, different interpretations tend to hang together in such a way as to make them alternative schemes or models of the relationship between man, education and society. However, one of the consequences of competing interpretations can be ideology and propaganda, as when any one interpretation emphasises its superiority and its distinctiveness and unconnectedness with other outlooks and so becomes resistant to innovation in its beliefs and ideas. As a result, statistical evidence and 'facts' are manipulated, distorted and selected to prove moral tenets that are assumed but which, in point of fact, are open to challenge. In this way, by clarifying the similarities and differences in contrasting educational ideals, the real points at issue, the educational dilemmas, can be identified. It will then remain to decide who makes the choices between the alternatives, who is influential in this respect and on what bases decisions are taken.

Defining the situation

In attempting to understand the significance of contrasting interpretations of education, it is necessary to examine a number of factors in the immediate situation that make it possible for conflicting educational ideals to compete for influence.

It is possible that a complete analysis of the ideas involved in progressive and idealist conceptions of education would require a consideration not only of the statements of leading protagonists but also an examination of their individual experiences, their own early education and their relations with parents and friends. Thus Brian Holmes (in Lauwerys, 1968) has suggested that an idealist's opinions might be explained in terms of an unconscious desire to dominate, whereas the progressive's views might be symptomatic of a refusal to face adult life. Such suggestions might sometimes contain some truth. But the importance of such unconscious motives might be questioned if conscious reasons which seem adequate to explain actions and opinions also exist.

Motives for sympathising with any particular conception of education have little to do with the validity of the arguments involved. But motives for promoting any particular argument are closely associated with the 'success' of any particular interpretation. Of use in this connection is the notion of the 'social circle' (Znaniecki, 1940), that is, the audience or the public to which any particular definition or set of definitions appeals. Educational choices rarely appeal to the total society; rather, they are taken up by selected segments or publics. Specific social circles bestow recognition, provide material or psychic income and help shape the educational theory as it develops.

There are a number of different explanations of the appeal of different interpretations of education to various sections of the population. One of these relates acceptance or rejection of an educational theory to the notion of interests or vested interests involved. Any situation includes its own definition of what are legitimate interests. Thus, conflicting conceptions of the structure and functioning of education also involve competing interests. There will be disagreement between parents and teachers who see their own and their children's best interest as lying in the idealist conception of education, and those parents and teachers who see that the progressive conception is to their advantage. Those who see advantages for themselves in any particular theory are likely to be critical of any alternative proposals, primarily because such proposals will entail a loss of perceived relative advantage in terms of prestige, wealth, authority or whatever. As a result, they will see far-reaching conspiracies and moral depravity in competing theories. At the same time, they will defend the rationality and morality of their own conception, emphasising the advantages and playing down the disadvantages as transitory defects. Thus, any group will defend its own interest, often by distorted and selective arguments, and will be less than objective in its appraisal of the opinions of others.

Problems of this kind have been considered by, among others, W. G. Runciman (1966). Runciman's explanation is intended to describe how changes can occur in people's conception of what is desirable in the workings of the (education) system. Although intended as an explanation of how people's notion of social justice can change, Runciman's theory of relative deprivation can be extended to the education system. Basically, his argument is that 'objective' or 'real' inequalities or injustices are irrelevant to ideas of the appropriate operation of systems. The important variable is the element of perceived deprivation or privilege. Thus, feelings of deprivation or privilege are not related to the absolute degree of deprivation or privilege as measured according to some overall standard by a 'disinterested observer'. Rather, they are a question of the reactions of the deprived and the privileged themselves and these are largely governed by the standards of comparison invoked. The standard of comparison or the comparative reference group refers to the point against which individuals compare their own position.

Relating this to the education system, in any situation there will be a category of people who are discontented and a category of people who are contented with the workings of the education system. These groups of people cannot be distinguished in terms of any absolute amount of deprivation or privilege involved but rather in terms of the standards of comparison which they draw. Thus, they will consider themselves relatively deprived or relatively privileged, depending on whom or which group they use as their point of comparison. For example, a teacher in a grammar school might consider himself relatively privileged if he uses teachers in other educational establishments as his standard for comparison. Another grammar school teacher, invoking other professional groups such as, say, doctors, as a point of comparison, might consider himself relatively deprived. In an education system that is highly selective, many people may believe that it is the 'natural order of things' for some to achieve in the education system and in society, and for others not to achieve. They may consider themselves relatively privileged because they are invoking some other standard of comparison (they may consider that to have health, strength or happiness is more important than to achieve). Or, they may be displacing achievement into areas not related to educational sources of prestige: for example, by holding a position of responsibility in their church or local community.

It is important to note that in a highly developed industrial society with extensive communications (television, in particular) and with high rates of social and geographical mobility, the range of referents is widened and there is more opportunity for comparison with more privileged groups. As a result, the aspirations of the population in general are raised. More people demand more from the education system, and ideas concerning the 'proper' role of education diversify.

Heightened aspirations and self-interest are obviously important in considering the appeal of various conceptions of education to different sections of the population. However, justification for the acceptance of any particular definition is usually in terms of the 'social good', the 'national interest', 'social justice' or 'the good of the individual'. Thus, the choice is justified as a rational one (or 'rationalised') in that it relates appropriate means to desirable ends. In other words, adherents to any particular view of education justify their position because they believe their solution of the educational dilemmas, their particular definition of education, together with their specific conceptions as to the nature of man and the genesis of knowledge, and the relation of all educational factors to the total society, to be the best possible solution. But self-interest can exert a strong influence on rational choice.

Finally, it is necessary to examine the sort of social situation that is conducive to competing interpretations of education, and the kind of factors that are likely to give advantages to certain interpretations rather than others. It might be hypothesised that in relatively stable societies the educational system will work towards the general stability. Stable societies are those where there is a high degree of status crystallisation and an individual's rankings on the various hierarchies of prestige, power, wealth, etc. tend to be directly correlated, and where change of any kind is slow and likely to be undesired. In such societies, education's main function will be to socialise the new generation into the attitudes and beliefs of the past and the present by teaching respect for culture, learning and achievement such that the new generation will be motivated to take over and fill the occupational and social positions necessary for the continuation of the society.

In contrast to this, in societies undergoing more rapid social change, where there is social and geographical mobility and consequently a low degree of status crystallisation; where there is an extensive system of communication, widening the range of referents for comparison, then the education system will be included in the more rapid general changes. Individuals and groups will continually redefine what the education system should be doing and what the society should be aiming for, and rejecting as unfair or inappropriate what was formerly accepted as right. In such a situation, there will be a number of contrasting approaches to the goals, structure and functioning of the education system. The implementation of any particular approach will depend largely on the general social and political climate which can be influenced by a wide variety of factors, the most important being wars, economic stability and prosperity. Also, success will depend on the attitudes and characteristics of those who make political decisions and on the influence exerted by organisations such as the universities, teachers and local authorities on those decisions. For the present, it is sufficient to note the importance of change itself in this respect: change can have a profound impact on people's conceptions of what is possible and what is tolerable in the education system.

An additional element that can be identified in the social situation as conducive to competing interpretations of education, is the fact of the limited perspective and lack of awareness of the large majority of the population. Not everyone has the opportunity or the desire to acquire first-hand knowledge of the working of the education system. In this way, it is possible for many people to imagine or to be told that certain educational and social values are better realised than they actually are. Of course, people may hold ideas that are contrary to their own interests. Alternatively, the extent to which social and educational values have been realised can be exaggerated by underestimating the extent to which they could be realised. In such circumstances, commitment to an educational ideal could be rationalisation, but this is not necessarily so since rationalisation implies that the truth is known but cannot be admitted.

Where public awareness or interest is limited, either deliberately by withholding or selecting information, or because of public apathy or indifference, then one particular approach to education—the approach endorsed by the political leaders—is likely to be implemented and maintained. Increased awareness is accompanied by growing realisation of differences in interpretations of desirable ends and appropriate means. But growing awareness and diversity of interpretations have other consequences. Individuals and groups commit themselves to realising certain aims which are included in their conceptions. They try to convince the uncommitted and to gain adherents by simplifying complex situations. Statistics are manipulated, facts are selected and educational alternatives are presented as *a priori* statements. In this way, different people, variously informed and variously committed, can be persuaded to cooperate towards the same goal. Protagonists define the situation and justify a particular course of action. The interests of the group call for the deception of those less involved, by the condemnation of antagonists and what they stand for, and the promotion of sectional ends and interests by ostensible selection and generalisation.

Depending on one's own values and the particular circumstances, it is possible to say that public 'awareness', competing interpretations of education and the oversimplification of complex problems that result, sometimes help in achieving desirable social change, sometimes facilitate undesirable social change, and at other times facilitate desirable or undesirable resistance to social pressure for change. But in attempting to view contrasting approaches to education from a less involved standpoint, which does not include trying to prove 'them' wrong and 'us' right, the question of truth or fact does not admit of a single unequivocal answer. Different approaches, like all complex cognitive patterns, contain many propositions. True propositions coexist with false ones. One particular approach will often point to important features and draw attention to variables previously unperceived or unacknowledged. But any one approach can also be in error about many aspects. In addition, emotional and often eloquent pieces of writing aim to convince and gain adherents but they can also result in a hardening of boundary lines and a reaction in kind. In so far as support of any particular conception of education requires that eyes be shut to new evidence or that evidence is immediately rejected as partisan, such attitudes interfere with processes of communication between groups and the attainment of compromise alternatives.

However, it is not enough simply to realise that contrasting approaches to education use distortion and selection to present their case. Furthermore, it is not enough to spread 'correct' facts. Wise policy making and rational action require that each group exposes, examines and seeks to understand dispassionately its own distortions and those of other groups. If we are to attempt to understand competing and conflicting ideas in education, it is necessary to simplify and, at the same time, to categorise the ideas. By doing this, it is possible to identify the particularity and therefore the limitations of each view. Simply to reveal the divergent angles of vision obviously will not result in universal harmony. But clarification of the sources of differences would seem to be a precondition for any sort of awareness of the limitations of one's own views and at least the partial validity of the views of others. This, then, will be the first task. By taking a number of key concepts in education, contrasting definitions and interpretations will be analysed to assess their essential similarities and, at the same time, their crucial points of difference. A similar analysis will then be made of the various approaches to school structure and organisation to see how these are related to the definitions of basic concepts. Finally, the connection between a particular view of education and the desirable relationship between education and society will be examined. This clarification will make possible at least a working agreement on what are the points of similarity and, likewise, what are the real educational dilemmas. Thus, although there is, and will continue to be, disagreement on ultimate values, it is possible to build up a discourse within which the opposing factions can communicate and discuss without ambiguity.

2

Intelligence and the educated man

The fact that some children perform better than others in intelligence tests is not a matter in serious dispute. Similarly, the related point, that some groups within a population perform better than other groups, cannot be challenged. In America, for example, the average Intelligence Quotient (IQ) of the black population is about fifteen points below that of the whites. In Britain, the mean IQ of the professional class is twenty to thirty points above that of the unskilled labourer class. What are matters for dispute are, firstly, the reasons that are put forward for these differences, and secondly, the precise nature of what is being measured; in other words, the relationship between measured IQ and intellectual (and other) abilities. There are a number of different and often contrasting models of intelligence and each has rather different implications for the education process. In addition, theories of intelligence tend to be adjusted to a particular conception of education and a particular view of the relationship between education and society. But first, it is necessary to examine the dispute concerning the biological and socio-psychological bases of intelligence and the relative weights to be given to different factors.

The heredity/environment debate

Terms such as 'heredity' and 'environment' are both abstractions that refer in each case to a complex variety of factors. 'Heredity' usually refers to the process of transmission of qualities, characteristics, etc. through human reproduction and the biological mechanisms of genes and chromosomes. In addition, there is a second level of transmission of human characteristics which might loosely be called 'social' or 'socio-cultural' and operates through the mechanism of habituation, learning and symbolic communication. These two processes of transmission, genetic and communica-

17

tive, occur in several different kinds of environment, geographical, biological, cultural, interpersonal. For this reason, any individual is just as much a 'product' of his environment as he is the result of the two kinds of dynamic transmission. The problem has been oversimplified, however, such that the hereditary or bio-physical environment is seen as contributing one set of factors, and the socio-cultural environment another set of factors out of which the individual develops. Further oversimplification occurs when the problem is put in the form of the question: which are the more important determinants of intellectual ability, hereditary factors or environmental factors? This is a misleading question as Kingsley Davis has shown (1948).

> In the first place, there is no such thing as 'the' environment. There are many different environments, and what is environmental in one sense may not be so in another. Thus, from the point of view of genetics, the body is an environment in which the reproductive cells multiply and receive nourishment, whereas from the point of view of ecology the body is what the environment surrounds. In the second place, the question wrongly assumes that environment and heredity are somehow opposed, so that if one is important the other cannot be. Since, however, organisms are perpetuated through germ cells and nourished in an environment they obviously depend on both of these factors. In the third place, the question makes a comparison without stating the terms of reference. The term 'important' is used, but important for what? Finally, the question confuses necessary with sufficient conditions. A necessary condition is one that must be present if another factor is to operate. From the standpoint of a biologist a woman speaks because she has the organic capacity (it is assumed that somebody teaches her to speak). If, however, the question is why she speaks Chinese rather than some other language, this is not a sufficient explanation. Speaking Chinese is a cultural datum; and only a cultural explanation—in this case, the fact that she was reared in a Chinese Society—can give a sufficient answer.

But the oversimplification of the problem into the heredity/environment controversy has important consequences for education. It results in questions being framed in a particular way. Are the children of certain races and certain social classes 'innately' less intelligent than the children of the white middle class? That is to say, is the superior ability in IQ tests and the greater educational achievement of certain groups of children a result of their being born with more intelligence or is this a result of less tangible factors in their 'environment', factors such as upbringing, parental relationships, material conditions, peer group contact, school conditions, in fact the whole life style of the group? There is no reason why different abilities should not be as much a product of differences in inheritance as of differences in environment. If the children in several generations of the same family have been successful educationally and occupationally, the fact can be ascribed to heredity reinforced by 'assortative mating' (or the tendency of people to choose marriage partners of similar ability and success). But equally important is the fact that parents can give educational advantages to their children in ways other than through their genes. Occupations are frequently transmitted from parent to child but never by biological transmission. There is a tendency, however, for opinions to divide on this issue; many idealists would stress the importance of innate ability and intellectual potential while acknowledging environmental influences; many progressives, on the other hand, would emphasise the overriding importance of home and school in the development process and would treat innate potential as an unknown (often unknowable) variable.

Models of intelligence and intelligence testing

Attempts to study intellectual development have been of two main kinds. The first has its roots in British empiricist philosophy which was based on a belief in the infinite plasticity of man, and finds its way via some of the doctrines of the utilitarians into modern behaviourism and learning theory. This approach is exemplified particularly by the work of Piaget (1926 and 1932), when he describes the child's changing attitude towards rules and social controls. Jerome Bruner, an educational psychologist, influenced by Piaget, has done much work into the development of intellectual capacities. He identifies a number of stages of mental growth as a foundation for his theory of learning. Freud, too, could be included in this tradition with his instinct-based personality theory. Freud was concerned to stress the irreconcilability of the demands of society and the interests of the individual, which has rather different implications from the approach of the behaviourists in general. Different again are the consequences resulting from the work of what might be termed the positive tradition in sociology. Such an approach makes it possible to conceive of human development in non-moral terms such as 'role' and 'class'. The individual develops in order to participate in a factually existing social order and to pass judgment on this order is irrelevant or inappropriate. Other attempts to study the development process have been of a rather different kind. These studies have tended to concentrate on the differences in personality types, group characteristics and achievements rather than the similarities from which a general learning theory begins. In one sense, this might be conceived as a function of the level of generalisation but it is from such an approach that a framework has been drawn for the present heredity/environment controversy. Both approaches, developmental and comparative, have contributed to the growth of theories of intellectual development and models for intelligence testing. Views as to the proper function of education, particularly with regard to realisation of the ideal, the educated man, have tended to remain implicit.

Early attempts to study intellectual development usually concentrated on either environmental or hereditary characteristics. One of the early environmentalists was J. F. Herbart (1776-1841), a German psychologist. Herbart's psychology was a development of Hume's view that the mind is not active at all, but that consciousness and thought consist of the association of ideas. As Peterson (1952) explains, Herbart expresses this by saying that what happens when we think is that 'an idea rises above the threshold of consciousness'. Once an idea has entered the consciousness, it forms, by 'fusion' or 'complication' with other ideas, an 'apperception mass'. Ideas which are rich in their associations are, of course, readily absorbed into such apperception masses and held in the consciousness; those which have few or no associations with our other ideas 'mean nothing to us' and so quickly 'fall below the threshold of consciousness'. Ideas therefore differ in their 'presentative activity' according to their vividness for different minds, and this vividness depends on the extent to which they are attachable to already existing apperception masses. The main difference between his view and Hume's, therefore, was that Herbart thought of ideas, not as dead pictures arranged in patterns, but as dynamic entities struggling for admission to the consciousness.

Herbart, like Helvétius, stressed environmental factors since it was part of his theory that the mind of every child at birth must be presumed to be a complete and equal blank, all subsequent differences being due to the different ideas which rise to consciousness and form apperception masses. His influence on contemporary progressive ideas about motivation is obvious since Herbart stressed that the teacher's function was to feed the mind with ideas which would build up into apperception masses. Everything depended on the subject matter being presented to the pupil in such a way that it would rise vividly into his consciousness and, joining with ideas already there, form new apperception masses.

In other words, ideas must be presented in such a way as to secure the pupil's interest and attention. Contemporary progressives have moderated Herbart's view that man is *simply* the sum of all the ideas which have been fed into him since birth, but his theories have had considerable influence.

During the nineteenth century, advances were made by the 'heredity' school. The earliest work in this field concentrated on racial difference and was motivated by a desire to explain why certain nations or races were more successful in terms of material progress than others.

J. A. de Gobineau (1816-82) wrote a four-volume work, *Essai sur l'inégalité des races humaines* (1853-5), in which he argued that lack of initiative and courage followed upon racial interbreeding and that this accounted for the decline of nations or civilisations. He asserted that races were unequal, some being capable of progress, others quite incapable of becoming civilised.

Gobineau's theory was developed in a different fashion by Sir Francis Galton, a cousin of Darwin, and by his follower Karl Pearson. Both men were social statisticians who helped to develop ideas of the normal curve of error and its relevance to the physical characteristics of man. Galton established a laboratory in London to study physical and psychological data. He held that individuals were unequal in physical and psychological characteristics and that in any society these characteristics were distributed in accordance with the normal curve. He asserted that such differences were largely the result of heredity, and he went on to outline the 'science' of eugenics which aimed to study the development and transmission of these differences. His writing included *Hereditary Genius* (1869) and *Natural Inheritance* (1889).

During the early years of this century, important contributions to the study of inherited intelligence were being made in the field of psychology. Educational psychologists turned their attention away from teaching methods and concentrated more upon testing children for their suitability for different types of education. Most of the early work on intelligence testing was done in America, although fifty years ago Sir (then Mr) Cyril Burt was calling for an individual, native testing scale for Britain. Early work on intelligence testing began largely as a reaction against Herbart's theories and was developed primarily by the school known as Gestalt psychology. Exponents of this school held that the mind was always active in organising its experience in accordance with some intelligible 'scheme' of its own. In this process of ordering, the mind was capable of 'educing' new knowledge, this always being a knowledge of relations. This process of educing new knowledge was researched by Professor Spearman particularly in association with the mental activity of correlation. Spearman saw in the 'eduction of correlates' the type of 'thinking' by which all knowledge was acquired, and that this was, therefore, the highest type of mental activity. Hence correlations were included in intelligence tests.

Spearman's theories on the nature of intelligence were centred around the existence of a general factor, which he called 'g' and which was more general than the particular faculties of memory, reasoning, etc. In addition he identified a number of specific factors which he called 's'. The 'g' factor seemed to consist of some sort of mental energy or awareness. It was held by Spearman to be innate and inherited, reaching its full development by the age of sixteen or before. Skills in particular forms of mental operation were a result of 's' factors; these also were innate but, unlike 'g', they could be trained and exercised by particular kinds of education.

The development and sophistication of intelligence testing procedures over the past fifty years have been based on the assumption that a considerable proportion of ability was inherited and innate. This was necessarily so since intelligence tests were designed to measure that which was innate and to control for any environmental and cultural influences. For a number of years there has been a truce between extreme environmentalist and heredity factions such that both phenomena were acknowledged to be of great importance but that the relative importance of each was unestimable in the present state of knowledge. It was also implicitly assumed that the education system was to concentrate on environmental factors, particularly in making up defects in some educational environments, since without biological engineering, which no one contemplated, nothing could be done about hereditary influences. As a result of reasoning such as this, a number of environments were labelled 'deprived' and the task of early education was seen to be compensation for children from such deprived educational environments. Several compensatory education schemes were begun such as Project Headstart in America and in Britain a number of Educational Priority Areas were designated to receive increased financial assistance (see Chapter 4). Then, in 1969, the heredity/environment controversy was reopened by Professor Arthur Jensen's widely publicised paper on the inheritance of intelligence, published in the *Harvard Educational Review* (1969). In this paper Jensen was concerned particularly with racial differences in intelligence; he distinguished genetic and environmental components of intelligence and used an analysis of variance model to show that genetic factors accounted for as much as 80 per cent of intelligence.

Jensen did not argue that the poverty of the negro environment could not be part of the explanation for their poor performance. He argued that it was not a sufficient explanation on its own, and he cited results from a number of studies carried out in the last fifty years in several different parts of America which indicated that abilities varied across both race and class lines. Naturally Jensen was challenged. The criticisms usually took the form of an assertion that on the figures available the gap could just as easily be the result of environmental factors. P. V. Smith and R. Light have replied to Jensen in this vein in subsequent editions of the *Harvard Educational Review*. In effect, such arguments claimed that the mass of evidence quoted by Jensen, however suggestive it might appear, did not add up to scientific proof of anything. In this country, Jensen's argument has been taken up and advanced by Eysenck (1971) among others. Newspaper articles and television programmes have brought the debate into prominence.

In this way, the question of the nature of intelligence has become an important issue in contemporary educational thought. For the most part, opinions on this issue have divided along the general progressive/idealist split. Most progressives question the *meaning* of Jensen's statistics and conclude they mean little except that the two complexities of factors are inextricably intertwined. Much of the progressive argument has centred on criticism of the testing of intelligence. Progressives have been concerned to stress how, in their opinion, concentration on intelligence testing and the automatic association of a high IQ score with brightness and potential achievement have put the education system in a strait jacket for the past fifty years.

Idealists have placed considerably more faith in the predictive powers of IQ tests. This kind of testing and its attendant theory of the relatively constant level of the IQ, genetically determined and inherited, together constituted important principles justifying the selection of pupils for an education adapted to ability. Sir Cyril Burt, for example, following Spearman, identified a single universal factor of intelligence, 'g', at the top of a hierarchy, above a number of less important but more specific group factors such as verbal ability, numerical ability, etc. Although he conceded a small part (about one-fifth) to environment, this general intelligence factor was largely determined by heredity. As evidence, Burt cited many examples of research, including work in orphanages and studies of identical twins. In *Black Paper* II he reported that the correlation between the intelligence of identical twins separated early and brought up in different environments was as high as 0·7 or 0·8. For non-identical twins and ordinary siblings brought up together the correlation was usually about 0·5. However, as Owen and

Stoneman point out (Rubinstein and Stoneman, 1970), the correlation for identical twins brought up together is between 0·9 and 0·95. This suggests substantial influences from both genetic constitution and environmental conditions.

Stott and Lewis (1966) have cast considerable doubt on the value of twin studies in general by showing how untypical twins are. D. H. Stott in his article proposes that congenital factors be considered as a third set in addition to genetic and environmental factors.

Professor P. E. Vernon (1969) makes a similar point:

Apparently, the infant brain is particularly vulnerable to dietary deficiencies during later pregnancy and early feeding, say from three months before to six months after birth. The damage occurring then to the brain cells from lack of protein, proper vitamins and other crucial elements may be irreversible; it cannot be made up even if the older infant or child is relatively well fed.

Many progressives have seen social deprivation as all important in depressing intelligence. (Again, twin studies are used, this time to show large differences in the educational achievements of identical twins separated early in life and reared apart.) Deprivation in this sense did not necessarily imply a lack of physical needs or even a lack of affection. It was more a lack of 'appropriate' attention and intellectual stimulation of children by their parents. Working class parents did not talk to their children as much as middle class parents, or in a way that helped them to develop the vocabulary and the concepts which were so important if they were to make progress at school (Bernstein in Rubinstein and Stoneman, 1970). Initial child-rearing differences (Newsons, 1963; Klein, 1965) were further emphasised when the children started school. Continuous parental interest, concern and manipulation of the system were a feature of middle class rather than working class educational life. Teachers' expectations of their pupils was another factor that could affect their IQ and attainments, and in general teachers expected more of their middle class pupils (Rosenthal and Jacobson, 1968).

The best form of evidence for the environmentalists' cause would be the achievement of changes in IQ as a result of deliberate changes in the environment. As yet such evidence is slim. A number of special education programmes have been started in Britain, designed to improve the intellectual environment of underprivileged children. But it is too early to assess how effective they have been. In the United States, an assessment of a number of these programmes showed an average gain in IQ score of only five to ten points. Obviously, immediate dramatic results cannot be expected from such compensatory educational programmes. A few hours a day in even the best equipped of nursery schools cannot hope to compensate for any adverse environmental influences that will have been at work continuously throughout a child's life.

The progressive view on the nature of human intelligence is well summarised by Professor P. E. Vernon (1969):

> We are not entitled to say that hereditary factors produce particular characteristics.... What we can say is that man's capacities are not determined by his internal structure to the same extent as those of species lower in the evolutionary scale; they are built up in him to a greater extent through stimulation and learning.

Following on from this, the idea that an IQ measurement can provide an accurate assessment of a child's ability to absorb a given amount of knowledge is regarded as completely outdated. To quote Vernon again (1968):

> We must give up the notion of intelligence as some mysterious power or faculty of the mind which everyone, regardless of race or culture, possesses in varying amounts and which determines his potentiality for achievement. In particular, we must relinquish the will-o'-the-wisp that, by avoiding verbal tests of intelligence and resorting to tests based on abstract materials like progressive matrices or performance tests, we can eliminate cultural handicaps and so arrive at a true measure of potential. There is no such thing as a culture-fair test, and never can be.

An alternative view of intelligence is the multidirectional, multidimensional model described by Professor J. P. Guilford (1967). Guilford is critical of the hierarchical model of Burt which is dependent on the reality of a 'g' factor (a general inborn quality of intelligence). To quote him:

> Unfortunately, the most telling evidence against a universal factor in tests of intellectual performance is the decisive number of zero correlations that have been found when tests have been sufficiently varied in kind and have been constructed with good experimental control and when other experimental controls have been exercised in testing operations.

Guilford's own model (1965) assumes that:

> There are numerous unique intellectual abilities (but not an

enormously large number), that collectively can be regarded as composing intelligence.... And with respect to the nature-nurture issue, there are, moreover, some indications that learning may well make substantial contributions to those abilities.

His theory distinguishes some 120 distinct intellectual factors, of which over eighty have been identified to date. Like 'g' of the hierarchical models, these special abilities are probably determined genetically. Guilford is reticent on this point, but, nevertheless, the implications are profoundly different. Owen and Stoneman give an illustration (Rubinstein and Stoneman, 1970, p. 84):

Supposing only 4 of the 120 factors turn out to be completely independent, of significance intellectually, and determined independently genetically (a deliberately cautious view), then, ignoring other genetic accidents and perinatal and environmental effects, it would follow that only one person in sixteen, or less than 7% would be below average in all of these abilities; or put another way, over 93% of people would be above average in one or more of the abilities. With more independent factors more people would excel in at least a few things. Although they might lack the particular combination of factors to perform certain intellectual tasks well, they would almost certainly have potentiality in other directions.*

The hierarchical and the multidimensional are alternative models of the nature of human intelligence. Each has rather different consequences as far as the process of education is concerned, for each contains implicit conceptions as to the goal of education in terms of the desirable characteristics of educated men. Idealists see the task of education to be the development of the intellect of children in accordance with some generally accepted ideal. Children need to be equipped with essential skills such as reading, writing and arithmetic, and with necessary information, but their characters and minds also need to be moulded into a desirable shape that includes the characteristics of self-discipline and respect for intellectual accomplishments, as well as the achievement and understanding of complex intellectual skills. The hierarchical model of intelligence is fitting for such a conception of education and the character-ideal of the educated man. The 'g' factor, apparently consisting of some kind of mental energy or awareness, is innate, inherited and the basis of all intellectual skills and accomplishments. It is to be distinguished from 'lower' level factors, skills in particular mental operations which, although largely inherited, can be trained and exercised by particular kinds of education.

Progressive educationalists frequently react against such a view of education as character-training. Education, they argue, should be based on the development of the child; it is of paramount importance to relate learning to the child's stage of development and to his interests. The aim of education is the growth and development of individual potentialities. Children must be seen, not as erring adults, but as moral beings with a right to enjoy their own different world. The multidirectional, multidimensional model of intelligence is more in accord with the education-as-growth conception. It allows for the possibility that abilities in different directions could be valued equally as far as individual development is concerned (although the stubborn fact remains that society values particular ability combinations more than others).

It can be seen, therefore, that models of intelligence contain implicit assumptions regarding the end-product of the education process and the qualities of the educated man. Two generic types have been distinguished. Each has its own social principles containing fundamentally different assumptions about human nature and consciousness, and its own consequences for the transmission of knowledge. The first model represents the child essentially as object; education is concerned to realise the child's 'innate' potentialities. The second model is explicitly concerned with how the child actively constructs and arranges his knowledge of the world in his developing interpretational schema. The first model endows the child with 'intelligence', with a capacity of given power within which his thinking develops. As Geoffrey Esland says (Young, 1971, p. 88):

> He is a novitiate in a world of pre-existing, theoretical forms
> into which he is initiated and which he is expected to
> reconstitute. The teacher monitors his progress by means of
> 'objective' evaluation and he is differentiated from others by
> 'objective' criteria. The teacher is society's surrogate selector.

This model is founded on several assumptions about children and the human mind, most of which hinge on the attribution to them of a measurable quality called 'intelligence'. The debates about such education have centred on a 'more or less' argument. 'Intelligence', in the form of IQ, has been reified. I will suggest, also, that there is a connection between a reified view of intellectual status (including IQ and attainment) and the reification of school knowledge itself (see Chapter 3).

One of the main features of the second model is a preoccupation with subjective experience and its composition, in which man is an active not a passive creature. Emphasis is on the construction of thought forms through sensory and linguistic ordering. Through the grasp and manipulation of various superordinates which organise the multiple zones of knowledge, the child develops a series of inferential chains which enable him to bring under control increasing quantities of data. Central, therefore, is a view of human learning and human sociation generally as being derived from a dialectic relationship between consciousness and socially-approved, socially-distributed knowledge. This dereifies the child, knowledge and intelligence. Because the area of socially-approved knowledge is allowed to be diverse and open-ended, the pupil is expected to find some cognitive attachment between himself and his school projects; he is expected to become committed. 'Intelligence' gives way to 'curiosity' as the desirable educational characteristic. School deviance changes from 'unintelligence' to unwillingness to cooperate and emotional neutrality (Geoffrey Esland in Young, 1971).

The ideas contained in these two alternative models have a history of their own and have developed in response to, or in reaction against, particular historical and structural features of society. It is to these historical factors, and to the development of the ideal of the educated man, that we now turn.

Growth versus character: the end-state

The ideal of the educated man has undergone change over time. During the many centuries that education was under the control of the church, the educated man ideal was defined in terms of piety and otherworldliness; spiritual development was the ultimate purpose of education. The term 'gentleman' represented the individual skilled in worldly matters, cultured in the arts and adept at sport and hunting.

During the period of English colonialism, the characteristics that education was designed to produce underwent a change. Education was the moulding of a socially desirable type. Boys were to learn those qualities of character, courage, kindness, self-reliance, obedience, industry and intellectual honesty which would enable them later to live as good members and leaders of the community. This was the educated man ideal embodied in the English public school system. The spiritual development of the individual was not forgotten. The public school system was confident that the individual reached his true spiritual development in the Christian-gentleman-leader ideal, which was at the same time the type which society required (Peterson, 1952).

When Thomas Arnold was headmaster of Rugby (1828-42), he introduced a number of changes that had a profound effect on all public schools in England. In turn, the public schools affected the whole secondary and primary education system of Britain, the USA and many developing countries. Arnold's aim was for Rugby to be a community with its own schoolboy standards, the highest of which the schoolboys were capable, but at the same time not adult standards. The typically public school practices which Arnold encouraged such as organised games, prefects, the house system and corporal punishment were introduced to enable boys to learn qualities of character and leadership such as self-reliance, courage, industry and fairness.

But even before Arnold, attacks had been made on the notion of education as character-training. Rousseau had protested against the lack of respect shown to children (*Émile*)—'Childhood has its own ways of seeing, thinking and feeling'—and by stressing the necessity of understanding a child's nature he opened up the whole field of educational psychology. His protest was taken up by Dewey in America, who made substantial contributions to progressive educational thought and practice. As a pragmatist Dewey was more concerned with immediate issues that have a practical bearing on human interests than with long-term considerations of purpose and value. His famous saying (1916), 'the education process has no end beyond itself; it is its own end', has been quoted often and is indeed a key statement summarising his thoughts about education. He regarded education as growth, mental, moral and physical. As a result of such thinking, increasing importance was attached to taking account of the stage of development of children, to waiting until they were 'ready' to learn what had to be learnt from experience. Their interests had to be built upon and they had to become 'agents of their own learning'. Children were to be active participants rather than passive recipients in the education process.

In commenting on such a view of education, A. D. C. Peterson (1952) has suggested that:

> In its simplest form [this] is the belief that there are no eternal truths either moral or intellectual; that 'good' and 'bad' conduct means simply socially convenient or inconvenient conduct; that truth means what works in practice, and that knowledge is only real to the extent that it affects our present conduct.

The progressives, in revolt against what they considered to be the old authoritarian system, have erected this view of education as growth into a universal panacea. But, in fact, it offers no solution.

Criticisms of education as growth and development are both substantive and moral (Hirst and Peters, 1970). Substantive criticism refers to its general indeterminacy with regard to aims and content, for it is difficult to see what 'growth' amounts to as an educational aim. But more than this, contents and curriculums should have regard to the demands of society and the experience we have gained from man's attempt to understand the world as much as regarding the child's interests and needs. The moral criticism of this view of education is that it tends to obscure the fact that a teacher must have views as to what constitutes good or bad development, and that he is in a position of responsibility with regard to the directive functions of teaching. In the teaching situation decisions about what is desirable are being made, implicitly or explicitly, all the time. The moral ideals of autonomy or self-determination are implicit in the notion of 'growth'. But the progressives are assuming that these are somehow innate characteristics that it is the function of education to actualise. Reacting against the idealist conception of education which was seen to be the inculcation of a stock of information, skills and a definite character ideal, the progressives stress qualities of mind such as 'critical thought', 'creativeness' and 'autonomy'. But as P. H. Hirst and R. S. Peters show well (1970, p. 31):

> They do not sufficiently appreciate that these virtues are vacuous unless people are provided with the forms of knowledge and experience to be critical, creative and autonomous with.... Being critical must be distinguished from being merely contra-suggestible, just as being 'creative' must be distinguished from mere self-expression. Both presuppose mastering a mode of experience and being trained in techniques. Both also presuppose a mastery of some body of knowledge. It is pointless being critical without some content to be critical of; autonomy, or following rules that one has accepted for oneself, is an unintelligible ideal without the mastery of a body of rules on which choice can be exercised. The romantic protest, in other words, presupposes some kind of a classical background.

In so far as we are concerned with educating people, we are concerned with bringing about desirable states of mind. Different conceptions of education are attempts to specify in more detail what these desirable states of mind ought to be. There is some difference of emphasis here in that progressives stress self-determination, creativity and critical thought, while idealists would put rather more emphasis on depth and breadth of understanding, self-discipline and certain intellectual achievements and accomplishments. But there is surely room for manoeuvre and compromise here. What must first be acknowledged is that mental development is neither a matter of the unfolding of potentialities from within nor a stamping of something from without. The work of Freud and Piaget has shown that both of these models are too simple by far. Maturation theories explain nothing except in the case of physical development. But statements of character ideals which can be brought about by competition and coercion are no more satisfactory. Abilities and characteristics develop as a result of the interaction between a child, his genetic constitution and his physical and social environments. Development is the process whereby the individual structures his own perception of the environment. This development is assisted by stimulation from other people as well as by contact with the objects perceived, but it cannot be directly taught. Thus, development is the interaction of a mind, which is characterised by its capacity for classifying and discriminating, with its environment.

A second point that has to be acknowledged is that the concept of development implies value judgments, and this is necessarily so. Some ideal conception of a human being is presupposed. Teaching can only be carried on in the light of some ethical view about what qualities of mind are desirable human characteristics. This is the case whether the character-ideal is made explicit and can therefore be explained and justified or whether it remains implicit and therefore unexplained and unjustified. In other words, education has to be related to some evaluative conception of man.

But it is meaningless to talk about the educated man ideal apart from the historical and structural aspects of the society. Changes in educational outlook parallel the changes which a nation undergoes in the course of its history. The social need of the times determines what will be included in the curriculum. Education changes with cultural ideals.

In the mid-nineteenth century, where the public schools were concerned, one of the main needs in the rapidly expanding economy of the Empire was for rulers and administrators. At the same time, the study of the classics changed. Previously they had been valued for a particular style and elegance imparted to the scholar. Now a training in accuracy and precision, a mental training, together with a political literature, was sought from the classics and they were regarded as appropriate training for the vocation of ruling. A study of the classics was intended to produce men deeply concerned with the social and political problems of contemporary life, men steeped in philosophy and well able to generalise the mature thought of the ancient world in terms of contemporary necessity. In this way, a classical education for culture was 'reassimilated to the needs and conditions of a complex industrial and imperial society' (Clarke,

1940). The establishment of a rigorous system of selection for the higher civil service belongs to this phase of socio-cultural history. What was required was the production of professional civil servants who were cultivated and efficient at the same time. The 'cultivated' man was the ideal type preferred.

However, there were signs of change throughout the nineteenth century. Concern for 'qualifications' rather than family connections and the ability to quote Latin or Greek was beginning. Diplomas gradually began to supplement 'character'. The civil service examination, begun in 1854, introduced a 'professional' note. The criterion was to become 'education' rather than 'birth'. 'The not unreasonable argument for competition is that, in the absence of any other criterion, superiority of education affords a fair presumption of superior fitness for official labours' (Mann, 1850). A demand for the scientific and the technical, too, was heard and gradually brought about the development of night school technical education and a call for the reorganisation of secondary schooling. 'The demand was for a trainable expertise rather than for those qualities which came from having been nurtured within a certain environment such as the medieval institution of apprenticeship, the monastic school or the renaissance training in "courtesy" provided in "a great house"' (Bantock, 1963). The need for experts has meant that anyone of the necessary intellectual capacity can achieve both a high degree of 'expertise' and the success which our competitive society esteems. This century has seen a growing demand for clerks, managers, technologists and other recruits to the world of industry and business, recruits to 'superior' white collar jobs. Education has similarly been concerned with training the 'professional'.

Motivation: competition and need

As there have been different ideas about the end product of the education process, about the required characteristics of the educated man, so too there have been considerable differences of opinion as to the best way to foster the ideal. Coercion, fear of punishment and desire for reward, were for centuries the main techniques used to encourage children to pursue the goals before them in the education process. The thinking behind such a view was the belief that the average child would not, if left undisturbed, display much interest in academic pursuits that were too far outside his range of natural interests and understanding. The views of John Locke (ed. Quick, 1934) have been taken to embody such beliefs when he stated that:

Esteem and disgrace are, of all others, the most powerful
incentives to the mind, when once it is brought to relish them.
If you can get into children the love of credit and
apprehension of shame and disgrace, you have put into them
the true principle which will constantly work and incline
them to the right.

Rivalry and competition were considered important motivating
techniques. They were intended as a means to stimulate interest to
understand and to achieve. The reasoning was that children would
find interest in any activity when it involved competition with
other children; a desire to achieve the top of the form position
would encourage quicker minds and the fear of the bottom of the
form position would encourage the slower ones, certainly as much
as fear of corporal punishment. A form of internal competition
was a main driving force in the eighteenth century Jesuit schools
in France, where each boy had his appointed 'rival'. In Europe,
competition remains to this day the chief outside incentive to
interest. Its greatest supporter in England was probably Dr Butler,
the headmaster of Shrewsbury, who introduced into English schools
the complicated system of 'marks' which they have retained ever
since.

Rousseau was probably the starting point of the opposition to
the competitive approach to motivation. He stressed the undesira-
bility of a rigid curriculum, and he emphasised the value of activity
and experience for the child who was to be permitted to learn
according to his own needs which were mainly related to his stage
of (physical and mental) development. In the USA in the 1920s, the
Dalton Plan (Parkhurst, 1922) was produced as a systematic application of such ideas which aimed to provide a method of teaching
children as individuals according to their own needs, instead of
as a class. Each pupil entered into a monthly contract with his
teacher to carry out a syllabus or set course of study but was free
to distribute his time as he wished. Classrooms were renamed
subject-laboratories and the pupils had free access to them; in each
one there was a teacher to give guidance, suitable books and other
materials. Dewey renewed demands for education to be child-
centred and child-orientated, for an integrated curriculum, for the
breaking down of barriers between the school and the world outside and for project and discovery methods at all levels of education.
In *Experience and Education* (1938), Dewey contrasts the new
motivational methods with the old; he says that the new

opposes to imposition from above, expression and cultivation
of individuality; to external discipline, free activity; to
learning from texts and teachers, learning through experience;

33

to acquisition of isolated skills and techniques by drill,
acquisition of them as a means of attaining ends which make
a direct vital appeal; to preparation for a more or less remote
future, making the most of the opportunities of present life;
to static aims and materials, acquaintance with a changing
world.

Changes in technology also influenced attitudes towards children.
Where complex industrial processes were concerned, largely un-
trained children were less useful in the production process. Thus,
there was both an incentive to improve the quality of education
and the possibility of lengthening the period of childhood. In
addition, developments in psychology and psychoanalysis also contributed to the progressive case. Between the two World Wars, there
were signs of a fundamental change in attitudes towards children.
Teachers were showing a scientific interest in children and child
development. Ideas of educating a child according to his needs and
motivating him according to his interests, involved more than an
ordinary knowledge of children, and 'child-nature' became a study
that teachers actively pursued with psychology as their principal
guide. The study of individual children, their characteristics and
circumstances, became part of the teacher's task. Psychoanalysts
such as Freud, Jung and Adler were of considerable influence.
Obsessions, complexes and neuroses in children were noted and
their causes were discussed. These ideas provided support for the
case for self-expression and for freedom from restraint, for choice
and participation. Education, informed by psychoanalysis, aimed at
free, natural development through the prevention of repression and
its resulting state of unconscious conflict and neurosis.

Progressives have tended to overstate their case concerning the
contribution that play and natural development can make in education and claims have been made that are difficult to justify. John
Holt (1970a), for example, describes how the motivation to learn
in children is dried up by their school. Holt considers that 'the
school should be a place where children learn what they most
want to know, instead of what we think they ought to know'. The
theory implicit in such a picture is as follows: children have a
natural and insatiable curiosity; if teachers and others surround
them with materials and opportunities for the exercise and development of this curiosity, they will learn far more effectively
than if conscious attempts are made to teach them. In this way,
learning is related to the child's own needs, his stage of development; competition and coercion as motivational techniques become
redundant since the child's own interest is far more effective in this
respect.

34

This approach seems practical because of the psychology involved and the way it solves the problem of motivation in education. However, the idea that it does not matter what children learn so long as they happen to be interested and the content is related to their needs is both dangerous and nonsensical. It sounds morally enlightened as a result of its emphasis on the individual as distinct from attempts to mould children into a predetermined shape. It is nonsensical in that it disguises assumptions and conceals the fact that valuations are implicit in both the terms 'need' and 'interest' (Hirst and Peters, 1970, p. 32). Education is an intentional activity; it is not synonymous with learning, nor is it fulfilled by the mere satisfaction of curiosity. Furthermore, it is evaluative in the sense that not all knowledge is regarded as having equal worth. Education presupposes a view of what ought to be learned, even if this includes an experimental or discovery approach to problems of teaching.

In the psychology of motivation, it is accepted that theories of need cannot provide overall explanations; not all things are learnt because they are related to needs. Learning develops its own motivation as we become absorbed in the intricacies of a problem. But we know little about this cumulative motivation that maintains its own momentum when once initiated. The only thing we know is that it is very difficult to spark off in the large majority of children. There is also the problem of stimulating interest in different types of activity. Practising teachers know that there are always children who will never take part in certain activities unless directed to them. It is no solution to say that such a child has not yet reached the appropriate stage of development or that he has not experienced the required 'needs'. Teachers cannot be indifferent to cases where children do not fit into the theories of experimentalism and discovery techniques. Neither can they ignore important aspects of the environment such as the intimate connection between achievements in education and success in the occupational and social structure.

Obviously, interest is an important motivational force and existing interests, which may or may not be of educational importance in themselves, have led on to an interest in something which is educationally important. But the crucial motivational question remains, which educationally important activities are motivationally potent? Children have many interests and some are educationally undesirable. In addition, sustaining interest is an educational problem. It is not necessary to abandon interest as a methodological goal in teaching, nor do we have to reject totally theories of need-development if we are aware that 'need' always involves conceptions of value. As Hirst and Peters (1970) claim:

35

Our sympathies are with the progressives in their emphasis on motivational factors in education, to which they drew attention with their talk about the needs and interests of children. But our conviction is that this kind of motivation, which is crucial in education, is unintelligible without careful attention to its cognitive core.

This chapter has shown how there is a considerable amount of disagreement over a factor such as intelligence. Also, it has shown that there is little agreement about what education is trying to do and about what are the best techniques to achieve the goals that education sets itself. In each case we are faced with a dilemma, a choice between apparently equally validated alternatives, theories and ideals. We have seen also that sets of alternatives appear to hang together in such a way as to provide logically consistent theories of the education process. Thus, if education is defined in such a way, then it follows that a particular model of intelligence, a particular character ideal of man in society and a specific set of motivational techniques 'fit' with such a conception of education. We have distinguished two contrasting statements about education: one we have called 'progressive', the other 'idealist'. Obviously this does less than justice to the complexity of thought involved, but it is a useful analytical device enabling us to disentangle the educational dilemmas that pervade problems of decision-making and action.

This pattern will be followed in subsequent chapters. The aim will be to determine the dilemmas involved in how we regard knowledge and tradition and in how we view opportunities and selection in education. It will be seen that these dilemmas arise as a result of the juxtaposition of historical and contemporary values. Progressives and idealists have a totally different view of educational values, of the nature of man, the genesis of knowledge and the relationship between education and society.

---

* The statistics in this quotation (p. 26) imply a spurious degree of accuracy. If we suppose only four of the 120 factors to be independent, it does *not* follow that less than 7 per cent would be below average in all abilities. Only the general statement (with more independent factors more people would excel in at least a few things) is conceded.

3

The 'knowledge-ideal'

It has already been suggested that to 'educate' people involves a number of processes which are linked by some ideal conception, either implicit or explicit, of what would constitute desirable qualities in an 'educated man'. There is considerable disagreement concerning these desirable qualities, but any list of them is not infinite since the notion of education implies also that the qualities are valuable (in the widest sense, as being of value to the human race), and also that they include the development of knowledge and understanding. Our present-day conception of the educated man ideal is a recent development. Previous to the nineteenth century, the gentleman or the man of culture was the product of elaborate training and instruction; such a person had mastered and followed a number of gentlemanly skills and pursuits. But the term 'educated man' was not the usual one for drawing attention to this ideal; it was not used with the same overtones. The term 'education' covered a variety of processes including the rearing and bringing up of animals as well as children. In addition to the sort of instruction and training that went on in schools, 'education' also referred to the less formalised child-rearing practices such as toilet-training, getting children to be clean and tidy and to speak well. But these characteristics, although desirable and valuable (in terms of the comfort of fellow human beings), had little connection with knowledge and understanding.

During the nineteenth century, the notion of 'educated' as characterising the all-round development of a person morally, intellectually and spiritually emerged and 'education' began to be connected with the instruction by means of which these desirable qualities were thought to be produced. Also in this century, the distinction between education and training came to be made explicitly. The Greeks had distinguished education and training but the distinction had fallen into disuse until industrial developments of the eighteenth and nineteenth centuries made it relevant again. The highest ideals of education (pursued and maintained by the universities, in particular) were generally agreed to be the furthering of the method of free inquiry, the validation of scientific truth, the development of sensibility and understanding about the nature of human values, the broadening and deepening of knowledge and the maintenance of the intellectual, literary and artistic heritage of civilisation. Training, by contrast, was the process designed to meet the short-term, utilitarian needs of changing industrial society for manpower and recruits to fill new or vacated positions in the occupational sphere.

Much in this distinction depends on whether there is perceived to be any conflict between three goals: the furthering of knowledge, the development of the individual and the good of the community. Previous to the nineteenth century, the 'Christian gentleman' ideal was seen to be the answer to all three. The growth of industrialisation during the nineteenth century seemed to necessitate the separation of education and training in order to maintain the educated-man ideal in isolation from the short-term ends of profit and gain. The universities, true to their ideals, would have nothing to do with what they saw as 'training', and new institutions (technical colleges) grew up to meet this demand. During the twentieth century, further developments have challenged the universities' conception of the ideal of the educated man. A more elaborate utilitarian doctrine has emerged which sees education as an 'investment', as a subsection of the economy. Talent must be sought out and encouraged in order that it may be harnessed to the great national drive for higher productivity and bigger exports. The universities are finding this conception of education increasingly difficult to avoid as they become more and more dependent on state finance for their continued existence.

A marked dualism characterises our educational thinking at present: the high prestige given to public schools, grammar schools and the Oxbridge colleges reflects their continuing adherence to high standards of academic intellectual excellence detached from the economy and the occupation structure. We continue to distinguish between a liberal education and vocational training and to insist that liberal studies are included in the training of engineers, technicians and skilled craftsmen. Yet questions are still asked about the *over-production* of graduates and how they will ever be fitted into the world of work. Oakeshott (1962) points to 'that ominous phrase "university trained men and women"!' He goes on to assert the distinctive characteristics of an educated mind:

There are some minds which give us the sense that they have passed through an elaborate education which was designed to initiate them into the traditions and achievements of their civilisation; the immediate impression we have of them is an impression of cultivation, of the enjoyment of an inheritance.

Such a view involves a notion of education as a process designed to further the knowledge-ideal. This includes ideas regarding the characteristics desirable in an educated man. The knowledge-ideal must be maintained and furthered by the education of all to accept and respect the ideal through awareness of its worth; and the education of the able, those who meet its rigorous standards, to further the ideal. All this is seen as a process different from the process of 'training' a mind into 'a finely tempered, neutral instrument', and, therefore, needs to be carried on in different institutions.

The contrasting point of view sees education as a process of personal development where personal development and socially necessary skills are both seen as components in a single dynamic. In this case, a child, whose confidence or curiosity is constantly fostered, *wants* to acquire the skills he sees in his society and is prepared to apply the effort necessary to do so. Thus, according to such a view, the aims of both education and training cannot be distinguished. Each attempts (J. Hemming in Cuddihy, Gowan and Lindsay, 1970)

to release and develop each child's potentialities by
stimulating his courage to explore more of his environment,
under guidance, until he is at home in his world and has
acquired the skills and relationships necessary to be effective
in it.... Furthermore, every child needs to acquire the social
and moral skills: self-respect, consideration and concern for
others, the capacity to cooperate, the acceptance of
responsibility for his own behaviour and for the well-being
of the community.

There is no need to continue with the inefficient and wasteful 'binary' system of higher education since all institutions have the same educational goal.

It could be argued that the second conception is vague, indeterminate and omits knowledge from the education process. What does 'development' mean as an end of education? Surely education should be concerned with the history of man's attempt to understand and appreciate the world just as much as with the child's needs and interests. But it could be argued against the first conception that to see education in this way is stultifying and self-perpetuating. The knowledge-ideal only values the reproduction of the knowledge-ideal, and other 'potential' characteristics are either squashed or relegated to a secondary position in the value system. Thus to define education in terms of the knowledge-ideal is to manage knowledge in such a way as to maintain, or only slightly adjust, the status quo. This is to close one's eyes to the possibility of managing education to initiate necessary and desirable changes in the social system. It becomes important, therefore, to attempt to evaluate different theories regarding the management of knowledge and the consequences of this for educational systems (see Chapter 7). First, however, it is necessary to look at conceptions of knowledge itself, and in particular the persistence of notions of cultural worth in our evaluation of different types of knowledge.

The evaluation of knowledge: the cultural tradition

Once it is accepted that teaching is a directive activity and that different kinds of knowledge are of different worth both in terms of value for society and for the development of desirable qualities in the individual, the question becomes: which values should be encouraged and taught in schools and what is the principle behind the selection of certain values and the neglect of others? The justification of large numbers of our educational values is in terms of the moral worth of certain characteristics for the individual, the community and the society, based on centuries of experience and tradition. A small number of educationalists would reject such values on this ground alone by asserting that they are cultural anachronisms and that each age should develop its own values appropriate to the changed situation. This, however, is to take the notion of cultural relativism to an absurd extreme and to deny the possibility that one age may perhaps be able to learn something from another. A more important criticism of the evaluation of knowledge in terms of cultural traditions is the one that implies that such traditions in fact stem from the attempts of some power elite to maintain the status quo in general and its own privileged position in particular. Following this line of criticism, education becomes the indoctrination of all into the acceptance of the ideology of the power elite regarding the appropriateness of certain educational values. In this sense, education is the real opium of the people! Many educationalists are asserting a similar, although modified, version of this coercion hypothesis when education is criticised for maintaining the status quo rather than working towards changing attitudes, values and social structures.

It is not necessary completely to reject the worth of tradition in order to assert that, at the same time as having some value, tradition is also self-perpetuating and hinders the development of new conceptions of educational worth. In other words, although admitting that we can and must learn from tradition, we must also be flexible enough to recognise that, in a rapidly changing society, education must also be concerned with values and attitudes for a future which will be different from the present and probably very different from the past. We can accept this point while recognising the practical and theoretical difficulties of educating for a society, the characteristics of which are unknown and unknowable, and for individuals, if we do not recognise that at least some personal qualities are universally and absolutely desirable. In fact, more often than not, some notion of a desirable future society and of a type of individual is implicit when education is condemned as a conserving institution. It would be more intellectually honest, and indeed it would help those involved in teaching, if these aims and goals could be made explicit. But in order to understand and appreciate demands that education be an instrument of social change, it is necessary to examine the development of the cultural tradition and the knowledge-ideal that are still so important in education today while being the source of much criticism for those who would see the goals of education centred on the child.

In his *Theory of the Leisure Class* (1899), Thorsten Veblen described how, throughout history, productive work ranked low in the scale of prestige. Those at the top of the social scale lived from inherited property; they did not work for their income. Similarly with other activities, such as hunting, fencing, entertaining and even the learning of Latin, the aim seemed to be the unproductive expenditure of time. Other terms we owe to Veblen include 'conspicuous leisure', 'conspicuous consumption', 'conspicuous waste', all of which tie in with his central theme that conspicuous abstention from useful employment was the hall-mark of high status. The leisure class, by its behaviour and the standards it set, influenced the lower classes who tried to imitate them. The lower classes aimed for these leisure models and strove for their symbols and behaviour. Such a cynical view of the cultured man has been echoed by many contemporary critics who condemn the separation of education and 'life' and the distinction between 'high culture' and 'popular culture'.

Until the eighteenth century, when industrial developments initiated changes in the class structure of rural England, culture was the preserve of the aristocracy and knowledge was guarded by the universities and the church. Culture and knowledge were valued most highly for the type of character and way of life they produced. 'Good' music, art, literature and scholarship were the exclusive preserve of the aristocratic, ecclesiastic and university elites, appreciated by a minority and sponsored by and for them for reasons of prestige as well as enjoyment. In these circumstances, it was impossible to deny the existence of a realm of 'high' culture, with a privileged status in terms of the values it embodied and conveyed, and the culture of the rest of the population which was no culture at all in that it had no lasting worth.

There was no need to defend the supremacy of this elite culture until the industrial developments of the nineteenth century brought about large-scale changes, particularly in the value-system, with the ascendancy of more materialist values. Then critics began to deplore the persistence and spread of what they saw as 'low' cultural standards. The idealists of the nineteenth century, men such as Carlyle, Arnold and Ruskin, were critical of the changes industrialisation was bringing to England. They gave 'culture' a normative definition. Culture was a whole way of life but it included the *right* way of knowing and doing and it contained the best that had been thought, said, written and done. This ideal grew up largely as a response against the main currents of industrial society which were constantly threatening it. Culture needed guardians. Originally, these were to be found in some Platonic elite such as Coleridge's 'clerisy' or the 'regenerated aristocracy' suggested by Carlyle and Ruskin (Kumar, 1969).

It is important to make clear that the word 'culture' is used in two different senses. It can refer to a body of human achievement selected from the whole range of human activities and therefore implying a standard of moral or aesthetic excellence as against the more immediate demands of the 'market' or industrialisation. This was largely the sense in which it was employed by the nineteenth-century critics of industrialism and by present-day educational idealists. Or it may be employed in the anthropological sense of a whole way of life, where its usage is morally neutral and purely descriptive. This is the usage employed when contemporary progressives call for education to contribute to the development of a common culture. The notion of a common culture involves an attempt to bring all sections of the population to a similar level of consciousness, the assumption being that this will be a high one. But this common culture is not to be based on the universal acceptance by all of a high and low. It is associated with a call for social unity. It is an attempt to lay down a common experience agreeable to the unifying tendencies in modern democracy so that members of the community shall have a 'shared' understanding of their cultural heritage.

Contempt for popular culture and distrust of the notion of common culture and the cultural relativism to which it gives rise, are apparent in the distinction made by F. R. Leavis between 'representative' and symptomatic' works of art: high art is 'representative' of the culture that produced it, exploring the society and its values at their deepest level; low art is only 'symptomatic' of such a culture, incurious and uncritical about the values underlying it. High art is civilising precisely because of this honesty, this ability to get at the truth about the society. Thus, in the process of grappling with this high cultural tradition, we are extending both ourselves and our society.

Progressive critics of such absolutism, of such a hierarchy of cultural worth, see this distinction between high and popular culture as artificial and misleading. They suggest, instead, that we try to understand all aspects of culture through a sense of total culture, and that culture be used primarily as a means of refining that sense. As Krishan Kumar (1969) suggests, such a view of culture is both populist and egalitarian:

> It is equally illuminating to study pulp fiction, films,
> television and comic strips.... For an understanding of, say,
> English society's attitudes towards alien peoples, it is
> necessary to use both *A Passage to India* and the boys'
> weeklies, *Othello* and Ian Fleming's *Mr Big*!

This is not to suggest that we must study popular culture as the ideal. What is needed is for popular culture to be studied with the same attention and analytical rigour that have been applied to the study of high culture. The study of high culture is not the only way to increase our understanding of things human; popular culture is just as (and may be even more) vital in this respect.

Conflicting attitudes towards popular culture and towards the goal of a common culture give rise to contrasting educational theories and evaluations of the knowledge-ideal. With the growth of industrialisation, a different kind of 'knowledge' was developing, knowledge that was both practical and useful. The meaning of the term 'education' underwent a shift. The older and largely undifferentiated concept referred to the general process of bringing up or child-rearing to which the connection with knowledge and cultural worth was contingent. Increasingly, 'education' came to represent the process which developed desirable states of mind. The educated man ideal was defined in terms of deep knowledge of a specialised subject matter together with appreciation of tradition and understanding of items of lasting and significant cultural worth. These characteristics were universally and absolutely desirable. This conception of education has tremendous force today in the arguments advanced by idealists for whom knowledge, culture and tradition remain essential parts of the education process.

Oakeshott (1962) has distinguished two sorts of knowledge, both of which are always present in any activity: (i) technical knowledge which is the knowledge of technique that is involved in every art, science and practical activity. This sort of knowledge is often formulated into rules which can be learned, remembered and put into practice—that is to say it is the sort of knowledge that is susceptible to precise formulation; (ii) practical knowledge, because it exists only in use. It is not reflective and it cannot be formulated into rules. It is not esoteric (Oakeshott denies that there is anything mystical about practical knowledge) but it is traditional. (The term 'practical' knowledge is confusing here since in general use 'practical' is usually regarded as synonymous with skill or experience. Although this is partly what Oakeshott has in mind, in common usage it is not associated with tradition.) The two kinds of knowledge are distinguishable but they are inseparable, and any education process must of necessity involve an introduction to both kinds. The difficulty with practical knowledge is that it can never be taught, only experienced. Thus, in addition to teaching technical knowledge, education must also be 'an initiation into the moral and intellectual habits and achievements of society, an entry into the partnership between present and past, a sharing of concrete knowledge'. Oakeshott is critical of contemporary developments in education since these involve regarding practical knowledge as no knowledge at all. All knowledge is technical knowledge and education is seen as the training of minds in which mastery of technique is encouraged and is rewarded by power. The trained mind is contemptuous of the educated mind since the educated mind is not understood, nor is its worth appreciated. As Oakeshott says (1962; p. 31):

> Like a foreigner or a man out of his social class, he is
> bewildered by a tradition and a habit of behaviour of which
> he knows only the surface; a butler or an observant housemaid
> has the advantage of him. And he conceives a contempt for
> what he does not understand; habit and custom appear
> bad in themselves, a kind of nescience of behaviour. And
> by some strange self-deception, he attributes to tradition
> (which is, of course, pre-eminently fluid) a rigidity and fixity
> of character.

Idealists are concerned to point out that the kind of inspiration of which Oakeshott is critical has, in their view, invaded and begun to corrupt the genuine educational provisions and institutions of our society. Some of the ways and means by which, hitherto, a genuine (as distinct from a merely technical) knowledge has been imparted have already disappeared, others are obsolescent and others again are in process of being corrupted from the inside. The whole pressure of circumstances of our time is, supposedly, in this direction but most serious is the attack that is being directed against the universities. Even these great institutions are in the process of being taken over to satisfy the demand for technical knowledge and trained minds.

Idealists in the twentieth century continue to see education as the process which should select and socialise members of an 'intellectual elite' who would pursue knowledge ideals and maintain standards of cultural excellence.

T. S. Eliot's (1968) prescription for the intellectual elite is deliberately class-based; he is concerned to preserve the culture of the upper middle class since it is in the shared assumptions of this class that the culture of the society is to be found. The intellectual elite should include all who are in positions of power and influence in all fields—arts, science, politics—and they should be united by their class-based culture and outlook. F. R. Leavis (1948 and 1969) is also pessimistic about mass society and the effect it has had in the undermining of the powers of the intellectual elite. Leavis' concern is with the preservation of cultural standards but his conception of an intellectual elite is less class-based. He believes the elite and all aspirants should share a feeling of 'sensibility' and he suggests it is probable that this cultural sensibility could best be achieved by stressing the importance of a literary education for the intellectual elite. Such views on the nature of knowledge and culture, together with a hierarchical model of human intelligence, inevitably result in a Gilbertian conception of culture—only a minority can ever really appreciate the knowledge-ideal. Attempts to extend the knowledge-ideal to the mass of the population can only succeed by lowering the standards of the ideal. Similarly, any attempt to make culture widely understood and appreciated is bound to debase it. Karl Mannheim (1957) was in substantial agreement with such a view: 'Mass production and standardisation of goods to satisfy routine demands is one thing. In education, however, this principle can only make the lowest common denominator the universal norm.' For Mannheim, also, an intellectual elite was necessary to maintain and further the knowledge-ideal. However, Mannheim supported the idea of an elite selected by ability alone. This implied the education of some 'declassed intelligentsia'; the criteria of selection would be merit and intellectual excellence, and socialisation would be in terms of a character-ideal which would value the pursuit of knowledge goals and cultural worth.

In the nineteenth century the masses were frequently seen as a challenge to knowledge and cultural ideals. Carlyle envisaged them as characterised by 'blockheadism, gullibility, bribality, amenability to beer and balderdash'. During the twentieth century, idealists remain pessimistic about mass societies where industrialisation and bureaucratisation have resulted in increased alienation of the masses. Eliot (1968) held a restrictive view of the education of the majority and he implied that they only required a limited range of skills. He was highly critical of attempts to extend educational opportunity.

> There is no doubt that in our headlong rush to educate
> everybody, we are lowering our standards ... destroying
> our ancient edifices to make ready the ground upon which
> the barbarian hordes of the future will encamp in their
> mechanised caravans.

Eliot did not indicate the nature of the education that would be appropriate for the mass of the population but he was quite convinced that real talent would always manifest itself. Leavis has been much more concerned with the quality of the majority. During the 1930s, he conducted a campaign against school examinations in his concern for more meaningful teaching. However, an elite–mass dichotomy must be maintained, otherwise cultural standards and the knowledge-ideal would be destroyed. For example, Leavis (1948) justifies the maintenance of intellectual standards within a general democratisation of education:

> Nor should we be disturbed by the accusation that the
> view held up here is 'antidemocratic'.... The special
> education of the intellectual elite can only be undemocratic
> if it assumes that democracy entails a lowering of
> standards.

However, during the latter half of the nineteenth century and throughout the twentieth century, it came to be realised that education for the masses was necessary for economic, democratic and humanitarian reasons. At first, this remained 'education' of a limited and specific type, and the knowledge-ideal was not breached since real education was reserved for a small minority who were able to prove they had the necessary qualifying characteristics. Idealists today are much more guarded in their recommendations concerning education for a highly selected intellectual elite since the whole notion of 'elitism' has come to be associated with privilege, corruption, deception and resistance to change. Of the contributors to the *Black Papers*, none explicitly advocates privilege as such. Privilege has to be justified by other criteria: efficiency or maintenance of standards, for example. Bantock and Walsh would follow Leavis in most respects but they acknowledge that minor changes and adjustments are required to bring education into line with the spirit of the times.

Bryan Wilson (Reeves, 1966) is concerned that education is entering into a close relationship with the economy and that this is undermining the central concern of education which is cultural transmission. Wilson emphasises the need to preserve a respect for learning in our educational institutions and he is critical of the recent expansion of universities and their present concern with the vocational and the practical. (This expresses a general concern that market morality and efficiency criteria are taking over even in the citadel of the university; see Chapter 6.) The universities are very vulnerable to the student culture which is increasingly 'anti-cultural' and therefore undermines the central concern of such institutions which should be the transmission and maintenance of the knowledge-ideal and the socialisation of students into acceptance of and respect for certain intellectual values.

Thus, in the minds of many idealists, there is a continuing distinction between the real goal of education, which is the maintenance of the knowledge-ideal, and general education which is nearer to the process of socialisation, both being distinguishable from training which has the more immediate and practical goal of the world of work. Similarly, idealists distinguish a realm of high culture with a privileged status in terms of the values it embodies and conveys. The idealist tradition is profoundly elitist for it is of necessity only appreciable by a minority. This is because the nature of human intelligence is such that only a small minority are capable of appreciating this culture or maintaining the standards of the knowledge-ideal. Attempts to widen this appreciation or extend the knowledge-ideal can only succeed by debasing the tradition itself. Education is not just socialisation and training or even the 'flowering' of innate potential. High culture is not the same thing as popular culture. In each case, the distinction is essentially one of long-term value and purpose. While knowledge and high culture aim at 'truth', innate development and popular culture carry different values, values which are short-lived, economically inspired and, according to idealists, usually trite.

Idealists define the knowledge-ideal in terms of the intellectual, literary, scientific and artistic heritage of civilisation, and it is the duty and purpose of education to sustain and develop this heritage. In other words, the knowledge-ideal is something more than the transient individuals who, at any one time, take from and contribute to it. Oakeshott states (1962):

There is little doubt about the kind of knowledge and the sort of education which we should aim for. It is knowledge, as profound as we can make it, of our tradition of behaviour.... [A tradition of behaviour] is neither fixed nor finished;

it has no changeless centre to which understanding can anchor itself; there is no sovereign purpose to be perceived or invariable direction to be detected; there is no model to be copied, idea to be realised, or rule to be followed. Some parts of it may change more slowly than others, but none is immune from change. Everything is temporary. Nevertheless, though a tradition of behaviour is flimsy and elusive, it is not without identity, and what makes it a possible object of knowledge is the fact that all its parts do not change at the same time and that the changes it undergoes are potential within it. Its principle is a principle of continuity: authority is diffused between past, present and future; between the old, the new and what is to come. It is steady because, though it moves, it is never wholly in motion; and though it is tranquil, it is never wholly at rest. Nothing that ever belonged to it is completely lost; we are always swerving back to recover and make something topical out of even its remotest moments: and nothing for long remains unmodified. Everything is temporary, but nothing is arbitrary.

Many progressives, on the other hand, are critical of (or puzzled by) such a conception of the education process. Education must have as its goal the better development of the individuals for which it exists or, as Dewey said, 'education is its own end'. For progressives, the concept of 'education' has undergone a further shift. Education is seen as a number of processes linked with the development of states of a person that involve knowledge and understanding in breadth as well as in depth. But such a conception hesitates to define an educated man ideal or to define any characteristic as absolutely desirable. Rather, education is seen to be the development of what is intrinsic in each individual and it is also seen that many different characteristics are desirable and frequently of equal worth.

Such an educational philosophy was linked with a social justice appeal and an attempt to increase general awareness of what were perceived to be privileges inbuilt in the education system. In addition, education was helping to perpetuate hierarchical divisions in a class-bound society. As Raymond Williams says (1961a):

First, it weakens the principle of common betterment which ought to be an absolute value; second, it sweetens the position of hierarchy, in particular by offering the hierarchy of merit as a thing different in kind from the hierarchy of money and birth.

Instead education could be one of a set of institutional arrangements designed to achieve a common culture. By concerning itself with interpersonal relationships and by including the idea of solidarity within the fabric of its institutions, education could foster the conditions for a common culture.

There is less emphasis on any knowledge-ideal or any assumption as to a hierarchy of cultural worth. The knowledge-ideal is criticised by progressives for being a teleological explanation of the goal of education since it explains the importance of certain values in education by asserting that they are necessary in order to bring about some assumed desirable end. In other words, it explains one thing, the hierarchy of values in education, by showing that these have beneficial consequences for another, the knowledge-ideal. The principle objection here is that the end is not universally accepted. Progressives consider that at best the knowledge-ideal is not capable of being anything more than a persuasive definition of what education is all about. At worst, it tends to make education into a sausage machine (and a poor one at that) attempting to produce a standardised output of so-called educated men all in its own self-image. Education thus becomes a sterile repetitive process designed to place human units in a defined hierarchy of worth and value. Progressives argue that instead it could be actively creating a situation where unique individuals can develop according to some innate conception of worth and value which, presumably, would be undifferentiated.

In the final analysis, the debate centres around two issues: firstly, the question of the absolute and universal value of the knowledge-ideal as an educational goal above and beyond the necessarily more short-term considerations of the contributing individuals; secondly, the question of the possibility of mass appreciation of the value of the knowledge-ideal and of wider extension of its frame of reference and thus wider recruitment of contributors. With regard to the first question, this depends how knowledge is conceived in the reality of everyday experience. For the idealist, the individual recognises objects as being 'out there', the nature of the world is external and realisable. Objectivism is firmly embedded in the norms and rituals of academic culture and its transmission. Such a view implicitly presents man as a passive receiver. 'Bodies of knowledge' are presented for the child to learn and reproduce according to specified objective criteria. Educational psychology has been a powerful legitimating agency and rationalisation for objectivism. Through the procedures of psychological testing and school selection and evaluation, the 'good pupil' and the knowledge-ideal are reified.

The progressive view emphasises man's active construction of experience and there is a challenge to the static, analytic conception of knowledge. Progressives consider that the preoccupation with knowledge as object hides the complex problems of, and infinite variety in, its realisation. The status of knowledge as an entity is questioned. Knowledge is seen as subject to the interpretations of individuals as these are mediated through particular social processes. The focus, therefore, is diverted from how man absorbs knowledge so that he can replicate it to how the individual creatively synthesises and generates knowledge and what are its social origins and consequences.

Thus, there is a basic disagreement concerning the focus and purpose of education. Often progressives seem to imply that it does not matter what children learn as long as, in grappling with attempts to understand, they are extending both themselves and their society. It has been argued by idealists that this is an abdication of responsibility by progressives in that any education is bound to contain a specification of what an educated man is considered to be. But against the idealists, it could be argued that their singlemindedness of purpose can only result in education producing an image of itself, one that is permanently out of tune with the present-day needs and interests of individuals. All that can really be said is that the content of education can only be given form by some agreed conception as to what constitutes an 'educated man' and that this will be determined ultimately by an analysis in terms of desirability, interest and knowledge conditions. Naturally, arguments would have to be produced for emphasising some desirable qualities rather than others.

With regard to the second question, the possibility of mass appreciation of the knowledge-ideal and an extension of its terms of reference, idealists argue for rigidly maintained boundaries and standards defining the knowledge-ideal, and in this they relegate much learning, experience and skill to second-class status. Progressives acknowledge the difficulties of spreading mass appreciation and understanding but they do not concede that the attempt is necessarily self-defeating. Indeed, if mass appreciation of the ideal is unattainable, then the ideal can only maintain its position by the use of power and coercive techniques designed to inculcate deference and acceptance by the mass. Ultimately, the knowledge-ideal is more likely to be endangered by such measures. Progressives argue that its position would be better ensured by a widespread, albeit superficial, acceptance of its value.

The teacher's objective: knowledge guardian and children's guide

In an important sense, neither the progressives nor the idealists in education have fully come to terms with the 'new' phenomenon of mass education, either in economic, pedagogical or philosophical terms. It is important to hold on to the knowledge-ideal and high standards and to ensure that they are preserved within a system of mass education. It is also important to come to terms with the need to educate all the people and not just some of them. Idealists cannot ignore the problem of how all people are to understand and appreciate the value of the knowledge-ideal and yet accept that the majority of them will never understand and appreciate the ideal itself. Similarly, progressives have to recognise that if the needs and interests of the child are to be the main concern of education, then centuries of tradition of knowledge and excellence are in danger of being superseded by feelings of uncertainty that no one knows what is good, beautiful, valuable and scholarly. Once it is accepted that it is our collective responsibility to educate our young people, these problems cannot be ignored. There will be no release from the pressure of numbers. When is it practicable to end the period of general education? When the knowledge-ideal has been recognised and its future guardians selected? When development and growth can be seen to be well under way? Neither of these are very useful principles, yet decisions have to be taken about the school-leaving age and about progress to higher education. At the present time, less than one-third of each age group stays at school for a full secondary course; only 14 per cent of each age group enter full-time further education of which 8 per cent of the age group are in universities. There is considerable disagreement about increasing these proportions, and about raising the general school leaving age. This disagreement is obviously related to what education is seen to be aiming to achieve in terms of individual development, the maintenance of the knowledge-ideal and the general problem of progress and advance in society.

The role of the teacher revolves around all three goals: the development of the child in ways which are meaningful to him, the maintenance and the furthering of the knowledge-ideal, and the transmission of values and the socialisation of the child in terms of the expectations of the society. In trying to understand the role of any particular teacher, it is necessary to realise that the teacher's role is differently conceived by different sections of society and by pupils, headmasters and parents (Wilson, 1963; Floud, 1962; Musgrove and Taylor, 1969). The emphasis laid on these basic aims by any particular teacher will differ according to the teacher's specialist knowledge and how he sees his task, the age, sex and status of his pupils, and the kind of institution in which he teaches. For example, the infant teacher will be a socialiser rather than a man of knowledge and must concern himself with the development of the child in a way which is meaningful to the

51

child and relevant to his society. At the opposite extreme, the university teacher is first and foremost a man of knowledge concerned to develop and further the knowledge-ideal and to socialise students in terms of the character ideals of the man of knowledge; he is only indirectly concerned with the wider socialisation of students and with the 'needs' of society for occupationally trained manpower. (It is not intended to suggest that any individual infant teacher will not be interested in scholarship or that a university teacher will not be concerned with the welfare of students. It is suggested that where such teachers exist, as a result of their divergence from the generally accepted value consensus, they will experience more role conflict than their 'conforming' colleagues.)

Between these two extremes, there is a wide variety of interpretations of the teacher's role. The socialising goal, probably linked with the world of work, may be the dominant goal for parents and teachers in a non-selective secondary modern school. Staff and parents expect grammar and public schools to stress the knowledge-ideal and in doing this they are emphasising the schools' links with the universities and their isolation from immediate work goals. The technical college teacher has to be more aware of the world of work since his students and employers are likely to demand that his teaching is 'relevant'. He will see his role as socialiser in terms of work values and norms, and the knowledge-ideal will similarly be adjusted. The role conflict experienced by the liberal studies teacher in a technical college (Wilson, 1963) seems inevitable if value consensus is interpreted in this way.

According to such an analysis, role conflict is likely to arise wherever a teacher finds himself at variance with the dominant value consensus. The situation is complicated, however, by the fact that the knowledge-ideal may be more in accordance with the teacher's interests but, even more important, the knowledge-ideal is closely linked to the attainment of high professional status. With an occupation as highly stratified as teaching, the greatest prestige goes to the teacher whose role is closest to that of a university lecturer; the sixth form teacher, for example, who begins to treat his students as scholars (Warnock, 1970). A further refinement of this association between high prestige and knowledge-centredness is the fact that the specialist teacher who teaches one subject only is considered to be more academic, and therefore of higher status, than the general teacher or the teacher of 'peripheral' subjects such as domestic science, woodwork or physical education (Cannon, 1964).

Within any one school, there is likely to be a whole variety of different interpretations of the teacher's role and each teacher must work out his own compromise in terms of the needs and interests of the children he teaches, his own relationship with the knowledge-ideal and the kind of expectations that parents and others in the community have of the institution in which he is working. As a result of her empirical research into the importance of the teacher's interpretation of his role for the successful functioning of an education institution, Joan Barker-Lunn (1970) has distinguished the knowledge-centred teacher and the child-centred teacher in terms of their differing approaches to education. For the knowledge-centred teacher, the goal of education is the acquisition of information and the attainment of set academic standards; the teacher's function is to impart this information and his efficiency is measured in terms of his pupils' academic success:

The teacher whose approach to education was 'knowledge-centred' tended to favour the bright child, who he regarded as more worthy of attention, more industrious and well-behaved, and whose attitudes to school and work closely resembled his own. There was a tendency to regard the perceived deficiencies of the low ability child as due to factors beyond the sphere of school and teacher—poor attitudes to school and unsatisfactory behaviour standards were products of a poor home background; backwardness or lack of progress was frequently attributed to inherent laziness, and an apparent lack of interest or participation in non-academic school activities merely reflected the child's inability to do anything well.

By contrast, the child-centred teachers hold the view that the aim of education is to develop to the full the interests and potential of each individual child, and the education process is the 'drawing-out' of this interest and potential:

The child-centred teachers, while recognising differences in attitudes and behaviour between children of high and low ability, tended to explain these differences in terms of the disadvantaged position in which dull children found themselves, and to stress that maximum help and attention should be devoted to these children to counteract these disadvantages.... The more child-centred teacher tended to favour non-streaming as this would give a fairer opportunity to all ability levels, and as socially more desirable in that it avoids the segregation and 'labelling' of children which streaming implies.

Of course, Barker-Lunn was concerned with the primary stage of education and it is now generally accepted that at this stage teaching must be more orientated towards (not dictated by) the child himself and what is significant and meaningful to him. It is rather at secondary and higher stages of education that the dispute between those guardians of the knowledge-ideal and those who postulate child-centredness at all stages of education, becomes heated. It is at this point, also, that the relationship between education and ideology, between education and social change, and the question of the manipulation of knowledge become pertinent.

The question of the content and functions of the knowledge-ideal, and of the relationship between education and social change, cannot be adequately discussed without a consideration of theories concerning the manipulation of knowledge and to this question I will return (see Chapter 7). However, a number of points can be made. An encyclopaedic theory of education which the knowledge-ideal implies is, by itself, inadequate. The sum total of knowledge which forms our cultural heritage cannot be catalogued in any simplified form (as some 'core curriculum' theories tried to do). But to look exclusively at the child and define education solely in terms of what are alleged to be his needs and interests is no more adequate. By rejecting both of these extremes, it is possible to 'look to the traditions of learning itself and to the modes in which civilised man has learnt to interpret and understand his world' (Weaver, 1970). Looked at objectively, as elements of a culture, these areas of learning, disciplines or subjects that have become differentiated represent distinguishable bodies of knowledge. But looked at through the eyes of the learner, this knowledge-ideal can still be a means by which the learner achieves desirable characteristics, skills, attitudes and forms of understanding. What in one sense is a knowledge-ideal of absolute value in the outside world can also be grasped first as a realm of meaning or collection of abilities desired by the learner. The ultimate achievement of education is the development of the knowledge-ideal; the knowledge-ideal can only be maintained through the development of minds that can appreciate and wish to extend it; the more immediate task of education must be the development of such minds. Each educational situation will involve a reconciliation between the child's capacities and nature, the teacher's relationship to the knowledge-ideal, the expectations that diverse groups have of educational institutions and the perceived relationship between education and some desirable society. In so far as society exists in man as well as man in society, in so far as we are both the makers and creators of the knowledge-ideal as well as being conditioned by it, the reconciliation is in our hands.

4

Equality of educational opportunity and the idea of compensatory education

The educational problems raised by the notion 'equal educational opportunities' are many. The problems are not only of a practical nature: how to achieve equal opportunities; they are also conceptual: what do we mean by equal educational opportunities? All seem to stem from the general indeterminacy of our educational aims. The one concept conceals a number of different interpretations and each interpretation involves different consequences for the education process. The majority of educationalists will agree that in so far as differential educational achievements are not solely reflective of differential abilities, the education system is socially unjust, economically wasteful and the quality of intellect which education aims to maintain and improve is likely to suffer. There is disagreement, however, as to the priorities even within the generally declared aim of equal opportunity and, thus, disagreement regarding the best way of achieving this aim. Some educationalists see the most important task of education to be to give each child an equal opportunity to realise his potential. Others, although acknowledging the desirability of excluding 'irrelevant' factors such as class, income, religion, race or early handicaps, would stress the necessity of maintaining high intellectual standards for all to aim to achieve or otherwise running the risk of debasing the whole education process. Yet another factor, the 'needs of society', would be included by the realist who asserts that it is dangerous to attempt to consider education apart from its connection with the occupation structure. What can equality of educational opportunity mean in this situation of competing priorities and diversity of educational aims? The meaning that has been given to the notion of equality of educational opportunity has undergone considerable change and clarification is needed of how the different interpretations have developed and of the consequences of particular interpretations.

The 'pool of ability'

The English education system has been labelled 'elitist'. In its simplest form this means that the leaders of English society have been drawn from a small group of people who have used the education system to help maintain their position at the top. Thus, education was the sole preserve of the economic and political elites. The rest of the population were not educated in any way that was significant. It had been assumed that high intellectual ability was a rare commodity and that only a very small proportion of the population were capable of benefiting from higher education. In order not to waste the nation's supply of talent, this privileged group had to be separated from the rest of the population and nurtured by a special academic education which would prepare them for high positions in the social hierarchy. The development of hierarchical models of intelligence, and of the assumed link between high performance in intelligence tests and ability in general, gave credence to the view that there was a fairly strict limit to the supply of potential talent in the population. During this century, this intellectual elite of potential educated manpower came to be known as the 'pool of talent', the nation's intellectual resources or the 'pool of ability'. The theory behind the notion was, as previously stated, that an IQ of a certain level was needed to benefit from a particular kind of education. The 'pool', therefore, was made up of the numbers with an IQ above the minimal level. The value of the concept depended entirely on the selection criterion for membership of the pool, therefore, and this was ultimately a question of the validity of the various testing procedures employed. But social factors influence performance in tests of all kinds, including IQ tests; therefore, it is impossible to talk of a 'culture-free' test of real ability, although a great deal of research is being conducted into this problem (Watson, 1970).

Based on the notion of the measurement of innate ability, a number of attempts have been made to estimate for any society the size of its resources and reserves of talent. One of the most comprehensive attempts to estimate the pool of ability was that by D. M. McIntosh in the early 1950s (1959). The study followed through the secondary school histories of some 4,400 pupils who had been considered for transfer during 1950-7 in Fife, Scotland. The proportion of the group actually gaining the school leaving certificate was 6·3 per cent. By a study of the educational careers of the group, which attempted to assess potential at an early age, it was estimated that 11 per cent was the maximum number which could have been expected to attain such a standard. The theoretical estimate had been 16 per cent but the actual performance was bound to be lower as a result of immeasurable factors such as the influence of a good or bad home which operated against accurate prediction. McIntosh concluded, therefore, that, under present conditions, the maximum size of the pool of highly educated manpower would lie between 11 per cent and 16 per cent of the population. (He did suggest, however, how 'present conditions' could be altered.)

When use of the concept of the pool of ability was at its height, during the 1940s and 1950s, fears were expressed of the possibility of a decline in average intelligence within a nation as a result of the greater fertility of those parents with below average IQs. It was known that in this country, the families of the unskilled were larger on average than those of the professional class, even though both have larger families than the 'unproductive' clerk! Furthermore it was known that a child's intelligence score tended to decline with his position in the family. However, there was no evidence to support the contention that differential fertility can affect the general intelligence level (Maxwell, 1961). More recently, however, Jensen noted that, at the lower end of the IQ scale, the Negro birth-rate is particularly high whereas at the upper end of the scale it is particularly low. If heredity largely determined intelligence, such an imbalance in the Negro birth-rate could increase the gap between the average IQs of the two races.

A rather similar interpretation of the pool of ability is being made by contemporary idealists when they assert that 'more means worse'. Their contention is that the volume of the pool of ability is limited. Only a limited number of children are capable of benefiting from an academic, intellectual kind of education. Attempts to increase this number can only succeed, therefore, by lowering standards to the detriment of all.

Arthur Pollard in *Black Paper* II has challenged the argument that more students passing GCE O and A levels is proof of rising academic standards. His argument is that the marks are usually scaled each year not to an unchanging standard, but to a pass/ fail percentage, so that the additional passes, according to Professor Pollard, mean not that more means better but simply that more means more. Attempts have been made to answer this (Rubinstein and Stoneman, 1970; Cuddihy, Gowan and Lindsay, 1970). Sir Cyril Burt has claimed that standards in basic education are lower today than they were fifty-five years ago, although he admits that they have risen steadily since 1948. It is claimed that O level GCE maths questions compare unfavourably with questions tackled by children aged eleven and twelve some fifty years ago. University and college teachers faced with larger and larger numbers of students have commented on a general decline in basic education and in numerical and literary skills.

What underlies such criticisms is the assumption that human talent is rare, that only about 10 per cent of each age group can master a degree course, and that only something like 20 per cent can profit from advanced secondary education. Where such critics subscribe to the tripartite system of secondary education, this involves the further assumption that talent is of a particular kind. Such talent can be detected by various testing procedures at the age of eleven (or even earlier by streaming) and fostered by the subject-centred, disciplined education that is characterised in some of the long traditions of our well-established grammar schools.

The main difficulty in assessing the validity of such claims is the self-fulfilling prophecy element which is implicit when those who qualify for membership of the 'pool of ability' are separated from the rest to receive a concentrated academic education. Arguments in favour of segregation are usually in terms of good results from the segregated group, whereas, in fact, it is possible that the results are determined by the separation of the 'able'. In other words, far from determining the accuracy of 'pool' membership or the validity of the dividing line between the able and the rest, the process eliminates any possibility of wrong allocation showing itself.

A further challenge to the limited 'pool of ability' theories of the idealists was in terms of increased demands from the economy for highly trained manpower. An industrialised, automated society needed high abilities of many different kinds in large quantities. Pressure was put on the education system to increase its output of this commodity. Many idealists felt that the only way this could be achieved was to lower the standards of entry to the 'pool'; this would be achieved, they claimed, with a consequent decline in educational standards.

A rather different interpretation of the 'pool of ability' idea was to concentrate attention not on the supply of potential talent (regardless of what happens to the educated manpower produced) but on the demands of the economy for educated manpower (regardless of the resources of potential talent). This was more the interpretation placed on the concept in the USSR, and used to be the interpretation adopted by educational planners in France. In the case of France, a group of experts in various fields made calculations as to what society would be like in a generation's time; they then planned the education system accordingly. The *Commissariat Général au Plan* was responsible for producing five-year economic plans. In addition there were a number of specialist commissions, one of which was concerned with educational planning and this worked closely with the commission on manpower. In Britain, such planning is not undertaken. The Robbins Committee (1963), for example, adopted a compromise position on the question of whether the boundaries of the 'pool' should be defined in terms of the supply of, or the demand for, educated talent. At the time of Robbins there was no government philosophy on how to respond to the increasing number of applicants to university. The Robbins Committee refused to predict the number of university places in terms of the needs of the economy, and also refused to accept the idealists' assertion of a limited supply of ability. Instead, Robbins recommended that the number of university places should grow fast enough to accommodate a constant proportion of applicants; that is, the universities' share of the 'pool' should increase in absolute size as the proportion of qualified school leavers increased in absolute size, but that the relative size of the 'pool' to the proportion of qualified school leavers should stay the same, at between 50 and 60 per cent. Thus, despite increases in the numbers of qualified school leavers, the number of university entrants should have kept pace at between 50 and 60 per cent. In fact, the proportion has declined (Layard, Moser and King, 1969).

The initial reaction of the progressives to the 'pool of ability' idea was to reject it. Naturally enough, if IQ test results were seen as socially conditioned to a large extent, there was little purpose in attempts to measure 'innate' ability in order to assess the potential size of a nation's intellectual resources. Furthermore, if intelligence was as diverse as the progressives suggested, to impose a hierarchical model would be to beg the question and reject at the outset much of what could ultimately be regarded as talent. Attacks on the idea of a limited 'pool of ability' and on the testing procedures that were the criteria for membership, came from many quarters (Douglas, 1967; Hudson, 1966; Bernstein, 1970b; Yates and Pidgeon, 1959). Vernon presented evidence to the Robbins Committee to show that no calculations of numbers of capable students could be based on intelligence or other aptitude tests. Attempts were made to prove that fears of a decline in educational standards were unjustified (Jackson and McAlhone, 1969); that 'more' only meant 'worse' if the notion of 'average intelligence' was taken too literally and in fact that 'average' was a misleading concept when applied to educational standards. Halsey, reporting from the Organisation for Economic Cooperation and Development Conference in 1961, said that agreement had been reached to abandon the metaphor of a 'pool of ability'. Instead, concern was to be focused on 'the elaborate social and psychological conceptions of complex processes through which potential qualities are transformed into recognised and educated performances of many different kinds' (Halsey, 1961). Thus, from a preoccupation with genetically based 'ceilings' of ability, progressives recommend that our concern be with talent as a consequence of social experience. In this way the notion of a limited 'pool of ability' would give way in favour of less restrictive assumptions about potential intellectual capacity. However, for progressives to reject completely the notion of a 'pool of ability' was premature. Many progressives include the idea of a 'pool of ability' in their demands for compensatory education for the disadvantaged. This, however, implies a rather different notion of equal educational opportunities and the development of this concept must now be examined.

Equal educational opportunity: the recent history of a concept

During the early years of this century, equal educational opportunity was not a burning issue. After 1870 state-provided elementary education for all was more or less accepted as socially just, and it was assumed that the education system was successfully supplying the nation with a stock of talent. Grammar school scholarships for bright but poor children ensured that the system was fair and efficient in this respect. It was only comparatively late that the notion of nurturing the able for elite membership came to have any meaning or relevance at all, as is clear from the recommendations of the Bryce Commission or the 1906 report on higher elementary schools. However, a number of factors developed to challenge the complacency of this generally accepted state of affairs. The grammar school scholarships themselves indicated the amount of potential talent, so far untapped, among large sections of the working population. But the numbers of scholarships were fixed and the economic circumstances of the poor but bright pupils often prevented their being taken up. However, realisation was growing of the importance of education in an industrialised society as occupations were increasingly defined in terms of educational achievements. Individual aspirations and ambitions were heightened by a general increase in awareness as a result of wider communications and an extension of comparative reference groups (see Chapter 1). But it was probably the Second World War that marked the real turning point as far as education was concerned. The technological demands of the war pointed to the inadequacies of the education system in terms of the poor elementary education provided for everyone, in terms also of the lack of secondary and higher educational facilities for all but the very few and in terms of the completely inadequate provision for training and the tying of certain kinds of education with the world of work. Also the war, probably more than any other single identifiable factor, resulted in a change in attitudes such that social justice and public responsibility for a new and better world became priorities.

However, at the same time as demands for equal chances became more specific, interpretations of what equal chances involved became more confused. The 1944 Education Act was designed as an important part of the new deal, intended to stem the rising tide of criticism that education in England was a system for training the children of the elite to take over elite status. When the majority of local education authorities opted for the tripartite system of secondary education (grammar, technical and modern) after the 1944 Education Act, it was intended that the three types of school would be 'equal but different'. This was never achieved, but simply to talk in terms of the 'appropriate' level and type of education for any one child, as the Act did, means that it becomes less necessary to use the word 'equal' in connection with opportunity; there is no point in discussing whether the right opportunity for one person is 'equal' to the right opportunity for someone else.

Parity of prestige and esteem was never achieved in the secondary education system and so, at least in common usage, equal opportunity came to mean equal opportunity of gaining access to a grammar school. But when it is clear from the start that the majority of children must fail the test, equality of opportunity becomes unreal. Again, a strong element of luck enters the contest when the unequal provision of grammar places by the local authorities is considered. Finally, when the wastage from early leaving in the grammar schools, especially among the brightest working-class children, is taken into consideration, equal opportunity in the wider context is a non-starter.

There seem to be three possible interpretations of the notion of equality of opportunity in the educational context. The first interpretation of equal opportunity can mean that each individual should receive an equal share of educational resources, irrespective of 'potential ability'; all schooling should be of a standardised form. This would ensure unequal outcomes partly because individuals vary in their genetic potential and partly because the school is only one of the important forces in the upbringing and development of children. The distribution of genetic potential in a group of children is best assumed to be random, at least for the purposes of social policy, since in the case of a group, as opposed to individual comparisons, it is unknown. However, other social factors—motivation, parental interest, norms of aspiration, teacher quality, etc.—are known to be unequally distributed between social groups. Therefore, to equalise school facilities and leave the other factors untouched, as this interpretation implies, would not achieve equal opportunity.

A second interpretation of the notion of equality of educational opportunity is to treat all those children of the same measured ability in the same way, irrespective of environmental factors. This, in essence, is the way the tripartite system of secondary education has been operating. However, this interpretation comes under criticism on two main grounds. First, in terms of the social justice argument, it could be contended that since environmental factors play such a large part in measured ability test scores, to separate children on the basis of measured ability is largely a question of separating them in terms of favourable and unfavourable environments, regardless of real ability. Second, the needs of an industrialised, automated society are for high abilities of many different kinds in increasing quantities; we cannot afford, therefore, the tremendous loss of potential talent which ensues if we ignore environmental factors.

A different interpretation of equality of educational opportunity is needed, therefore, if we are to clarify our educational aims. With the concept of equality of opportunity, a new, a third, interpretation has already been made implicitly, although it has not yet been made explicit. Demands are now made, not for equal schooling (for with such unequal environments this would contribute nothing), but for positive discrimination in favour of educationally underprivileged children. The chief aim of compensatory education is to remedy the educational lag of disadvantaged children and thereby narrow the achievement gap between 'minority' and 'majority' pupils. Compensatory education has been practised on a massive scale for several years in many cities across the USA (Project Headstart, for example), and a call was made in the Plowden Committee's Report on Primary Education in Britain for positive discrimination for the educationally underprivileged areas. But before we can attempt to understand this new conception of equality of educational opportunity and its revival of the pool of ability idea, we need to examine the thinking behind demands for compensatory education.

Compensatory education

During the 1950s, there was a tremendous increase in research, particularly by sociologists, indicating that certain groups in the population were at a disadvantage in terms of educational achievement. Much of the research was concerned to show that the children of low social class (and in America, the black children of low social class) were outpaced in the educational race because their material and social environments were inadequate. New concepts were developed: 'cultural deprivation', 'restricted linguistic codes', 'the educationally disadvantaged' and, as a result, the notion of 'compensatory education' was introduced to describe the process of changing the status of children in these situations. A number of large-scale pre-school programmes and research projects, together with a multitude of small-scale intervention or enrichment programmes for pre-school children or children in their first years at school, were developed in an attempt to compensate for a deprived 'environment'.

In America, Project Headstart was launched by President Johnson in 1965 (Adam, 1969). The intention was to set up a comprehensive programme for pre-school children from economically and culturally disadvantaged backgrounds in an attempt to 'break the cycle of poverty'. The federal government provided 80 per cent of the cost, and the local communities organised and administered the project and paid the rest, largely through sponsorships from community action agencies and local government bodies. Children were eligible who lived within a neighbourhood which the local community had found to have a substantial degree of poverty, as defined by the Office of Economic Opportunity's criteria of economic deprivation. The Headstart programme started off with 561,000 disadvantaged children to 40,000 teachers and 500,000 volunteers. The project was designed as a two-part programme: year-round training for pre-school children from the age of three, and an eight-week summer school for the children about to begin primary school in the autumn. The programme consisted of five components: health, nutrition, education, parental involvement and social and psychological services.

In England, a number of studies (Douglas, 1967, 1968; Mays, 1962; Plowden, 1967) had indicated that in many areas, particularly the run-down, transition areas in the centres of large cities, children were working well below their educational potential and that many would have lower levels of attainment by the time they left school than they had at the age of eight. This seemed to indicate that the schools were a weaker educational force than a number of other 'environmental' factors such as parental interest and aspirations, family stability, money and the life styles of class and community. The Plowden Report on primary education made a number of recommendations on this problem. It suggested a two-pronged attack: the first part aimed at getting the government and local education authorities to improve the schools; but because the limitations of this line were recognised, the second part aimed at getting the local community interested enough to work towards improvement. The report recommended that a number of areas where children were under-achieving because of social handicap should be designated Educational Priority Areas (EPAs). The suggestion was that these areas should be given more money, teachers, buildings and equipment, but, further than this, Plowden wanted the schools to act as agents of social change. Plowden wanted the EPA schools to pioneer closer home–school relations and to experiment with community schools in an attempt 'to break into the vicious circle of deprivation'.

Six months after the Plowden Report was published, in 1967, the government announced £16 million of mainly primary school building in Educational Priority Areas for the years 1968 and 1969, and an element for replacing old EPA primary schools was set aside in the building programme for 1970 (Corbett, 1969). In February 1968, the Burnham Committee decided to allocate £400,000 for teachers in 'schools of exceptional difficulty', at a rate of an extra £75 per teacher per year. There was some difficulty over which schools were to qualify, but the Department of Education had designated 570 schools by early 1969. In May 1968, under the 'urban programme', some £20-25 million was set aside by the government for the four years from 1968. Education has come away with the lion's share of this, with most of it going to nursery education—10,000 new places have been provided in nursery schools (or 40 per cent of the previous state provision of nursery education)—and some to immigrant language centres and to teachers' centres.

In addition, the Department of Education and the Social Science Research Council jointly sponsored an Educational Priority Area action research project and £175,000 was granted for three years to find out the most constructive developments for EPAs. Projects were developed in five areas: Birmingham, Liverpool, London, the West Riding of Yorkshire and Dundee. The aim of the action research projects was 'to improve the educational experience of children in EPAs, to raise the morale of teachers, to strengthen home–school relations and to involve the school more closely with the community'. The research consisted largely in trying things out in the belief that this would demonstrate which were the effective methods, but the exact content depended on how each of the directors interpreted the aims and the ideals. In each of the action research projects, attainment surveys of children and attitude surveys of parents and teachers were carried out. In addition, each had a special language programme for pre-school children on the assumption that inadequate command of language was one of the most disastrous of the educational deprivations.

This notion of 'positive discrimination' in favour of underprivileged children is also behind the large research unit that has been established in Swansea, concerned with compensatory education and financed by the Schools Council. Research of a related kind is taking place at the University of Birmingham into the problem of the education of Commonwealth children. The most important question concerning all these compensatory education programmes is the problem of evaluation. It is too early as yet to come to any conclusions concerning the Educational Priority Area projects. However, experience so far indicates that such programmes can have only rather limited effects. Plowden recognised that the schools are not the most potent force in educational achievement: 'There is no reason why the educational handicaps of the most deprived children should disappear. Although standards will rise, inequalities will persist and the potential of many children will never be realised.' But in spite of this, it is a great deal easier ethically and practically to change the school than it is to tackle the family and the community. Apparently, Project Headstart in America is achieving no statistically significant degree of success; statistical evidence indicates that Headstart children score no higher than control groups of other deprived children. Naturally, there is considerable debate concerning these findings and they have been disputed (Smith and Bissell, 1970) on the grounds that researchers accepted extraordinarily crude terms of reference for assessing success.

While the statisticians continue to dispute such findings, a rather different line of criticism is being developed by Basil Bernstein (Rubinstein and Stoneman, 1970) and is concerned with the whole notion of compensation in education. Bernstein is concerned that

> The concept, 'compensatory education', has the effect of
> directing attention away from the internal organisation and
> the educational context of the school, and focuses our
> attention on the families and children. 'Compensatory
> education' implies that something is lacking in the family,
> and so in the child. As a result, the children are unable to
> benefit from schools.

In other words, to use the concept of 'compensatory education' is to distract attention from the deficiencies in the school and in the education process and instead to focus attention on deficiencies within the community, family and child. However, in so far as such compensatory education schemes usually involve changes in the organisation and immediate goals of the school, such criticism is not well-founded. Such schemes are developed largely because it is accepted that it is more desirable and morally defensible (as well as considerably more practical) to tackle the school and attempt to use it as an agent of social change.

Bernstein has a more fundamental criticism, however. Because certain children fail to come up to the WASP (White-Anglo-Saxon-Protestant) middle-class assumptions that school teachers and parents make regarding achievement and success in education, their language, culture and way of life are inferior, not just different; these children are 'deprived' and they are failures. We assume that our present educational yardsticks of achievements and success are good ones and appropriate for judging all children. The criteria of attainment that schools hold are accepted; and the competence of different social groups is measured according to their success in reaching these criteria. Having defined achievement in a particular way, if we find one group of children who possess attributes conducive to success in these terms, and a second group of children who lack these attributes, then the second group will be evaluated in terms of what it lacks compared with the first. In this way, the notions of 'deprivation' and 'compensation' confirm the existing state of affairs, confirm the one yardstick of achievement; and endorse one particular conception of education and evaluation of knowledge.

Only when there is agreement, therefore, as to what education consists of, are we entitled to establish a yardstick to evaluate success in these terms. It is increasingly obvious, however, that there is not one but many conceptions of education and evaluations of knowledge. If this is accepted, then it follows that we cannot distinguish between appropriate and deprived environments in terms of educability. There will be as many appropriate environments as there are conceptions of education. Bernstein concludes: 'It may well be that one of the tests of an educational system is that its outcomes are relatively unpredictable.'

Such a criticism brings us back, in other words, to the most fundamental question: what does education amount to? Although we can agree with Bernstein that we do not know what a child is capable of, as we have, as yet, no theory which enables us to create sets of optimal learning environments, it is necessary to disagree if this involves accepting undirected 'growth' and 'development' as educational goals. The teaching situation is a directive one in which decisions about what is desirable are being made all the time. Education is evaluative in that some kinds of knowledge and skills are valued more than others and, in so far as a child does not master these skills, he is handicapped and deprived. Similarly, we must also admit that so far as 'environments' are concerned, certain stimuli are known to motivate children and maintain their curiosity and interest more than others.

It is possible to say, therefore, that certain environmental factors are more conducive to the attainment of educationally desirable states of mind than others. We can accept Bernstein's comment that education should be flexible in terms of defining its end-product without taking this to an extreme position by saying that it is impossible to define *any* aims for education. We do not have to defend the superiority of a middle-class environment to admit that literacy, critical thinking, knowledge, sensitivity, etc. are worthwhile educational goals, or to acknowledge that parental interest, books at home and an 'elaborated' code of language are all positive factors in a child's environment that can give a child a head-start in achieving such educational goals. A child who is without such advantages *is* deprived compared with another that has them.

Every child has eventually to come to terms with a world in which growth and development in particular directions are allocated higher status, prestige, income and autonomy. Any child is likely to feel cheated when he enters the real world if the educationalists directing him have led him to expect anything else. If education is to be used to change society, it is not likely to do this by cutting itself off from the system of evaluation and selection that is crucial in allocating responsible and arduous positions. Education is intimately connected with society; knowledge is evaluated and teachers cannot escape their moral duty as guides and directors. Only when goals and aims are made explicit can they be openly discussed, criticised, ultimately agreed upon and techniques for their realisation debated. This is not to argue for a narrow educated man ideal; it is to reconcile all that has been found of value in the past with all that we anticipate might be of worth in the future. To recognise the difficulties in defining the object of education is not an excuse for allowing the means to obliterate discussion of desirable ends. Few people would argue that, because we are not clear as to what constitutes an optimum income, we should abandon all attempts to remove poverty. Likewise the fact that we are confused by the difficulty of our educational task is no excuse for abandoning attempts to remove at least the extremes of environmental deprivation. Compensatory education does not necessarily imply a fixed yardstick for assessing educational success; it is not comparable to a 'reform' or 'cure'. Rather, it represents an attempt to establish a basis, a grounding for each child, of universally agreed upon skills, learning and understanding, on the basis of which 'different but equal' may in fact stand a chance.

Equal educational opportunity: from social justice to criteria of efficiency

Compensatory education schemes and other projects attempting to equalise opportunities by enriching deprived environments have been subject to criticism from other directions. Many idealists claim that what is happening now is the replacement of 'equal opportunity' by 'egalitarianism' as an aim in education. Excellence and real ability are being subordinated to some sort of 'average child' guiding principle which implies condemnation of anything that begins to look like educational advantage. Real ability must not be explicitly encouraged or rewarded because this results in feelings of superiority and inferiority. As a result, there will be a levelling down of educational achievement: bright children will be 'held back' for the slow children to catch up. Idealists claim that such egalitarianism is based on the belief that all children, except for a few born with severe neurological defects, are basically very much alike in their mental development and capabilities, and that their apparent differences in these characteristics as manifested in school are due to rather superficial differences in the children's upbringing at home, their pre-school and out-of-school experiences, motivations and interests, and the educational influences of their family background. This belief, such critics maintain, contains an element of truth, but grossly distorts that element. Equalising educational opportunities must not involve equalising end-products, for excellence and intellectual ability should always be positively valued so that standards will be maintained and improved. Egalitarianism seeks to deny excellence by standardisation and uniformity. By asserting the moral rightness of educational egalitarianism, education itself, with its traditions of intellectual excellence and character ideals, is being destroyed. In theory, the egalitarian only wants all children to have equal opportunities to secure a good education. In practice, egalitarians go a good deal further than this by instinctively disliking any process which enables some children to emerge ahead of their fellows. Angus Maude claims (Cox and Dyson, 1969):

> The most serious danger facing Britain is the threat to the *quality* of education at all levels.... In the name of 'fairness' and 'social justice', sentimentality has gone far to weaken the essential toughness on which quality depends.... The motive force behind this threat is the ideology of egalitarianism.

Such criticism is already outdated, however. It seems unlikely that the principle of equality alone would ever have caught the public imagination. The contemporary ethos seems to hold little promise for those who seek a more egalitarian education structure. Although subscribing to the general aim of 'equal opportunity' in education, the basis of the argument has now shifted towards efficiency as the main criterion (Marsden in Rubinstein and Stoneman, 1970). As with other post-1944 plans for social change towards greater equality, the charge of waste of the nation's stock of talent proved more successful than the call for equality as a trigger for social legislation. Thus, egalitarianism has been replaced by efficiency and a return to the notion of making the most of the nation's supply of talent or 'pool of ability' in contemporary demands for equality of educational opportunity. The revival of the 'pool of ability' concept has involved a sophistication of the original interpretation and a number of assumptions are implicit which must be examined.

The new interpretation acknowledges that there is a genetically determined pool of talent in the population. The distribution of talent is normal in the total population and, in addition, the distribution of talent is normal in different groups within the population. Thus, there is a pool of talent to be found in every sub-group of the population. If we go further than this and assume that 'innate' intelligence is randomly distributed in all social groups, then the largest resources of potential talent must lie in the largest social groupings, not the small ones. In other words, although the mean IQ of the professional class is twenty to thirty points above that of the unskilled labourer class, there are many more in the working classes than in the professional class. Therefore, as many as 60 per cent of able children may come from the manual population.

In so far as the working classes are not producing their quota of bright children, this indicates that other factors are intervening. Environment is seen as a threshold variable in the development of ability; thus, environmental deprivation can keep a child from performing up to his genetic potential, so the aim is to counter this deprivation as far as possible. It is necessary to be clear, however, just what our aim is in this respect. Implicit in the new interpretation of equal opportunity is the principle of equal, or rather proportionately equal, outputs, in terms of the achievements of groups not individuals. The working class has the same proportion of bright children as the professional class but, because of their larger numbers, there are many more bright working class children in absolute terms. Thus, the extent to which equal opportunity is achieved is the extent to which these groups do achieve proportionately equal success rates. In terms of the total population, it might also be possible to estimate the reserves of ability. If we take account of the fact that IQ tests are class and culturally biased, there is a considerable amount of evidence to show that a combination of IQ, English and Arithmetic tests have reached a fairly high degree of precision as selectors. Such tests will always underestimate the amounts of potential talent, particularly within certain groups. But, if the general and the particular underestimations are allowed for, it should be possible to give some indication of the pool of potential talent. The difference between two sets of statistics—estimates of the pool of ability and statistics of achievement—will show how far we have gone in equalising educational opportunities since this could be studied in relation to class, race or any other differentiating factor.

This interpretation of the concept of equal educational opportunity is just as much open to criticism as the interpretations that have gone before. The most fundamental criticism is to question the relationship between IQ and talent or between achievement and talent. Alternatively, it is possible to question the assumption that intelligence is randomly distributed; perhaps certain races and classes are genetically less intelligent. The uproar following the publication of Jensen's article indicates how emotional is this field. But the fact remains that the random distribution of intelligence is an assumption. Just as important is the question, do we want equality of opportunity if this implies drastic 'manipulation of environments'? Of course children are manipulated now, when they are streamed or segregated at eleven, for example, and this fact must not be disguised in our general disapproval of social engineering. Many parents are willing to accept the decisions of 'those in authority' when they are told their child has not made the grade. Just how far is positive discrimination defensible or justifiable in the face of apathetic or directly hostile parents (for whatever reasons) in the belief that such children might make the grade? Such questions need to be considered prior to debates concerning the more practical details (difficult enough in themselves) of how to achieve more equal environments. It is possible to argue, for example, that segregation of children, for any purpose, even to discriminate in their favour, is likely to fail.

But does any of this matter to the devoted teacher who is battling away in a slum school attempting to give an educational start (the notion of an 'equal start' seems totally inappropriate) to young children with minimal vocabularies and experiences that have never included listening, curiosity, books or pencils or even the security of a warm, safe home and the love of parents? Probably not, and many would argue rightly so, since the arguments about educated man ideals or growth and development as educational aims must seem entirely academic. But this cannot be so for those who are responsible for initiating, framing and developing our educational theories and policies. Hidden assumptions, implications and consequences of diverse interpretations must be clarified and examined. With the current concept of equality of educational opportunity we seem to have collected together the disadvantages of a number of contrasting interpretations. We argue against the waste of talent, that cannot be defined and, many argue, should not be defined; notions of ability are related to the drawing of arbitrary lines on lists of results from testing procedures only partially valid. We argue for compensatory education at the same time as asserting that present educational achievements are a poor yardstick. We judge certain environments to be inferior while condemning any attempts to specify inferior to what and for what end. The concept of equality of educational opportunity has become a platitude universally accepted but almost completely misunderstood. Social justice will not be served by confusion over educational aims; moral responsibility cannot be explained away by promoting a means, a process to the status of a goal or a principle. But similarly, academic excellence will not be preserved by a narrow, inward-looking notion of what constitutes worth in a diverse and rapidly changing society. The confusion that at present exists among teachers, parents and children and in the structure and organisation of all our schools and colleges is a challenge to all educationists to elucidate their goals and clarify our progress towards them.

5

Selection in education

The question of the appropriate organisation of the education system obviously depends on the perceived goals of the system. In so far as there are differences in what are perceived to be the goals of education, so there will be disagreement concerning the organisational structure necessary to achieve these goals. One of the most significant structural features, about which there is considerable disagreement, is the importance of selection in education both for the education system itself and for the wider society. Indeed, Earl Hopper (1968) claims that 'the structure of educational systems, especially those within industrial societies, can be understood primarily in terms of their selection process'. It is not necessary to go quite this far but it is important to analyse the procedures, assumptions and consequences of selection.

In order to assess the appropriateness and necessity of selection in education, it is important to be clear what the terms mean. As an organisational arrangement, it is possible to subdivide the consequences of educational selection into two main parts: firstly, the consequences of selection as an organisational technique for the goals of the education system itself; secondly, the consequences of educational selection for the wider society. The first will be referred to as educational selection, the second as occupational and social selection. Although it is important to stress the *inter*-relationship between the two, it is also necessary to separate them since the principles and justification behind the two types of selection are different.

Educational selection is justified or otherwise solely in terms of the contribution it makes towards the furthering of educational goals or aims. In other words, it is as if the assumption had been made that selection in education was irrelevant to the occupational and social structure of society or, at least, that educational selection should be irrelevant to these structures and that we should operate as if it were. Educational selection is done according to educational criteria and is undertaken solely for the purpose of advancing the goals of the education process. The principle behind such selection is that children are chosen, counselled and directed according to their ability to fulfil the requirements of the education system and that it will be to the child's advantage and an advantage in furthering the goals of the education system for selection to be made. But, even within the limited frame of reference of the education system itself, important assumptions are involved. Educational selection assumes that educators actually possess the ability to measure potential aptitudes or actual achievements of children. This assumption has already been examined (see Chapter 2), and it was noted that a self-fulfilling prophecy operates whereby selection itself tends to bring about the consequences it predicts. Educational selection also assumes that the criteria of ability applied in schools, the various tests and examinations that indicate educational success, are related to some ideal conception of an 'educated man' and further that there is general agreement concerning notions of what being an educated man involves. Both of these assumptions can be challenged.

Occupational and social selection refer to the sorting and distribution of individuals between various occupations in the economic hierarchy and between various statuses in the social hierarchy, as a result of performance in the education system. The justification for selection in this case is that the formal system of education provides an avenue for social and economic mobility by selecting individuals according to its own educational criteria and, as a result of their performance, allowing them special access to the economic and social hierarchies. Many people think of education as the means by which occupational categories are achieved; education and occupation are related concepts. Similarly, occupation is the single most important indicator of social status and also of income and power. Thus, with many social positions, education and occupation, income, status and power are all interrelated. The principle behind basing occupational and social selection on performance in the education system is a meritocratic one. It implies that access to the most important, best paid, most prestigious and powerful occupations and positions in society should be reserved for those most successful in the education system and that this is somehow more socially just and efficient than, say, a system based on wealth and inherited property. Michael Young has described vividly some of the possible consequences of a totally meritocratic social structure (1958).

It is obvious, therefore, that the idealists and the progressives in education will differ in the way in which they see selection as an inevitable and important part of the educational process. In general, the division of opinion concerning selection is consistent with and predictable from different interpretations of intelligence and different perceptions of the educated man and knowledge ideals. The idealist will tend to support selection and its perceived academic advantages to children of high ability. If selection did not take place, the bright child would be held back, would be irritated by the slowness of the other children and would consequently become bored and frustrated. For the knowledge-centred idealist, satisfaction comes from seeing bright children reach a high standard of academic achievement. Competition seems to be necessary to motivate children to work for and achieve high academic goals. For the idealist, the arguments in favour of selection are primarily in terms of its effect on attainment and academic progress.

Just as high standards of achievement are factors of primary importance to educational idealists, so the social aspects of education receive most emphasis in the arguments of many progressives. Progressives would prefer that selection play a minimal part in the education process, that it was the child himself that did the selecting and that, in any case, selection was left as late as possible. While idealists regard segregation by ability as simply acknowledging a fact of life, progressives condemn it as artificial. The more child-centred progressive sees selection as working against the goal of education, when defined as the development of the potential of all children, since selection imposes a narrowly defined criterion of potential. Not to select would give a fairer opportunity to all ability levels. It would be socially more desirable in that it would avoid the segregation and 'labelling' of children which selection implies. Also, it would be more likely to foster cooperative as opposed to competitive attitudes among children. Thus, many progressives would disregard arguments about the best and fairest ways to select, about how to minimise strain on children and about how to avoid adversely affecting the primary and secondary school curricula and would ask instead, why select at all?

During the 1930s, critics of selection in the education system first began to be heard. Opposition to selection increased during the 1950s. At first the general unifying concern of the critics was the injustice of the system in operation. The principle of 'equal opportunities' in education became a source of mass as well as of powerful political support. But the broad base of the original campaign has become more diffuse. In the evaluation of particular schemes and schools, quite different and even conflicting views have emerged as to the best way to equalise educational opportunity. The early critics of selection emphasised the consequences of class barriers and inequalities in the education system. They suggested a number of organisational alternatives such as un-streaming, comprehensive schools, a common curriculum and flexible teaching methods to promote a new cooperative atmos-phere which would help the average and less able child and reduce injustice in the wider society. More recently, however, the critics of selection have tended to splinter with regard to the alternatives they advocate. Many who are critical of the consequences of educational selection would agree with the retention of com-petition, streaming, selection and specialisation, but would see the traditions of a middle class grammar school education extended to a much higher proportion of the population. Both social and academic justifications are advanced, and it is claimed that it is not necessary to choose between equality and preserving quality, since to increase opportunities would, at the same time, raise general levels of attainment. In fact, as D. Marsden (Rubinstein and Stoneman, 1970) points out, critics of selection today argue more in terms of the charge of wasting the nation's stock of talent than in terms of the original equality appeal. The Labour Government of 1964 and 1966 projected the image of efficiency first and equality second: 'The egalitarian principle, missing the first full-tide of socialism and washed up in a weaker form with Wilson's efficiency government, has probably spent its force.'

The advocates of selection in education have based their case on the need to get the best possible academic achievement, especi-ally from the very bright children. Selection is consistent with a subject-centred curriculum designed to train minds and characters in accordance with knowledge ideals. Evidence that there is a strong hereditary component in intelligence is seen to justify selec-tion, although care must be taken to exclude 'irrelevant' vari-ables such as race and class. But equality of opportunity must not be confused with egalitarianism which would mean the end of excellence, the destruction of the knowledge-ideal and a reinter-pretation of the concept of education which, in fact, would render it meaningless.

The issue concerning selection in education can be put in the form of the question: 'Should the education process include a selection function?' Answers to this question will vary as opinions vary on what education is all about; opinions will be consistent with views on the relationship between education and some desir-able social structure. Restricting ourselves to the question of educa-tional selection first (the principle of meritocratic selection, of the consequences of selection in education for the wider social struc-ture, will be considered later, see Chapter 7), it is possible to ask, 'Does selection in education promote educational aims and goals?'

If the answer is 'yes' it is necessary then to ask what is the best way of implementing this function and at what stage. If the answer is 'no' it is necessary to consider the alternatives to selection in terms of the promotion of educational goals.

The issue of educational selection is a crucial one for deliberations concerning the organisation of the school system. The selection debate usually centres around two focal points: firstly, the question of streaming; this has to do with the internal organisation of the school and the distribution and classification of children within it. Secondly, the problem of comprehensive or selective secondary schooling; this has to do with the organisation of secondary education and the distribution and classification of children into different kinds of school within a given area. Attitudes towards educational selection in general are important in understanding assertions concerning the structure and organisation of the school system.

Streaming

Streaming developed as a 'system' throughout the state schools, both primary and post-primary, in the 1920s and 1930s, to reach its peak in the early 1950s. Its origins can be traced to the beginning of the century, but it was particularly the reorganisation of the all-age elementary schools into junior and senior following the Hadow Report of 1926 that made this practically a universal method of internal school organisation. The Primary School Report of 1931 stated that:

> The break at the age of eleven has rendered possible a more thorough classification of children.... One great advantage of the self-contained primary school is that the teachers have special opportunities for making a suitable classification of the children according to their natural gifts and abilities. On the one hand, immediate treatment of an appropriate character can be provided for retarded children and on the other hand, suitable arrangements may be made for specially bright children.

In a school operating a streaming system, children within each year or age group are sub-divided into streams according to their ability or attainments. These may be assessed either by objective standardised tests, by school examinations or by heads' or teachers' reports. Streaming usually begins in the primary school. A majority of children are streamed at the age of seven, the large majority are streamed by ten, irrespective of the kind of secondary schooling involved.

76

The streaming method of grouping is based on the theory that intellectual potential is largely determined by heredity, that it is fixed and unchanging and that it can be accurately assessed at an early age. On this basis, streaming is clearly defensible. The aim is to achieve a homogeneous class of roughly the same level of ability and to teach the class as a class; as such, streaming is one of the most 'obvious' methods of internal school organisation. Children of different abilities can be allowed to progress at a suitable pace; the bright child is not held back and the slow child is not made to feel inferior.

During the course of this century, a number of the principles basic to the streaming hypothesis have been challenged. Perhaps most important in this context is the assertion that a child's intellectual skills and abilities are not fixed by heredity but rather are formed throughout the course of his life and experience, in particular through his use of language and his interaction with adults and 'significant others'. Such a theory of intelligence implies that to stream a child according to a prediction about his future intellectual development will determine that development to some extent because of the influence of the specific group of which he forms a part.

In the early 1950s, articles criticising streaming, frequently based on research findings showing its detrimental effect, began to be published in large numbers. Many progressives in education have made streaming a focal point of issue and have questioned the need for streaming, particularly in the junior school. A number of schools have been unstreamed and have reported benefits from doing so. The journal *Forum* has published many articles on the topic and has suggested methods of running a non-streamed school. (A number of these articles have been published in B. Simon (ed.) (1964).) Much of the relevant research has emphasised the arbitrariness of the streaming procedure and of the 'unconscious biases' in the streaming system. These biases are associated with the over-representation in A streams of girls, of middle-class children, and of those born between September and March; boys, working-class children and those born in the summer months are at a serious disadvantage in a streamed school system (Douglas, 1964; Jackson, 1964; Jinks, 1964; Sutton, 1967). Further criticism has centred on the operation of what has been called the 'self-fulfilling prophecy' element whereby the streaming process itself, far from determining the accuracy of allocation and the advantages of streaming, in fact eliminates any possibility of wrong allocation showing itself. These two criticisms, 'unconscious bias' and the 'self-fulfilling prophecy element', have formed the basis of much of the progressives' attack on the streaming process.

The main point at issue here between the progressives and the idealists comes down to a question of the relative advantages and disadvantages for children (and to a lesser extent for teachers) of teaching pupils of similar measured abilities together. Idealists stress the educational advantages of the increased motivation of the bright children and also the opportunities presented (although perhaps rarely taken up) for concentration of resources on those less able. Traditionally, progressives have emphasised the social justice and equality arguments for abolishing streaming, although contemporary progressives lay equal emphasis on the waste of talent that results from such premature selection.

Empirical research into the efficacy of grouping by ability is abundant. From the 1920s until the present day, there has been a vast amount of research into streaming both in Britain and in the United States, some in secondary schools, some in primary; some studied attainments, others studied non-cognitive aspects of education; some came to definite conclusions, others came to the opposite conclusions; most, however, came to no definite conclusions at all (Barker-Lunn, 1970).

There has been a great deal of research on streaming in the USA. But, despite its abundance, there is no clear trend which indicates the superiority of either streaming or non-streaming; different researchers have found contradictory results. In her review of important grouping experiments from the 1920s to 1959 in the USA, Ekstrom (1959) reports the generally inconclusive nature of their findings: thirteen studies found differences favouring streaming, fifteen found no differences or results detrimental to streaming, and five studies gave mixed results. Interest in the subject of grouping by ability has continued to grow in the United States. In the 1960s, two American Professors of Education, H. Passow and M. Goldberg, together with J. Justman, a director of New York's Board of Education Research Programme, initiated one of the most comprehensive research projects on streaming yet carried out (Goldberg, 1966). The authors say that before the research they were impressed by the 'apparent logic of the contention that a teacher can achieve better results with a group which is relatively similar in learning ability', but they were worried by the fact that available research provided no consistent support for this contention or any other. With the cooperation of fifty schools and 3,000 children in New York City the researchers designed a rigorously controlled and tested investigation into the effects of streaming. The specific purpose of the study was to explore the differences in achievement patterns, social relations, interests and attitudes among children of middle school years (eleven and twelve) when they were grouped and taught in various ability groups. Classes were arranged in many patterns—some narrowly streamed, some broadly streamed, some unstreamed. Each pupil in the experiment was tested at the beginning of the two years and again at the end.

For all the ability levels taken together, the greatest achievement gains were consistently associated with the broad ability range classes. However, the differences were generally small and for no one group were they significant in more than two or three subjects tested. Ability grouping seemed to have a more significant effect on self-attitudes than on achievement, but even here the differences were small. The type of grouping seemed to have no consistent predictable effects on either pupils' interests or their attitudes towards school. Nor did it have any effect on pupil attitudes towards peers of varying levels of ability. Goldberg concludes: 'In the absence of specific plans for changing the content and methods of teaching so as deliberately to provide the most needed and challenging learning situation for each group of pupils, ability grouping does not seem to make any appreciable difference.'

Such sentiments are echoed by Stuart Maclure in his review of a number of experiments in Sweden; Maclure claims that none of the results 'proves the merits of streaming or selective schools, but [they] draw attention to all-important questions of the teaching process itself. In other words, it isn't streaming or non-streaming that matters, but exactly what teachers and pupils are doing with themselves that counts.'

In December 1964, a conference of research workers from the United States, the United Kingdom and countries of western and northern Europe, was held at the UNESCO Institute for Education, Hamburg. The aim of the conference was to discuss the basis, operation and effectiveness of the various forms of grouping practised within these countries (Yates, 1966). The conclusions of the Hamburg conference were that research was plentiful but inconclusive. The reasons were that many of the inquiries had involved inadequate samples and were conducted over too short a period of time. Other reasons were the failure to take important variables into account or the limitations in scope of the experiments.

The fact that sometimes research favours streaming and other times non-streaming would seem to indicate that factors other than particular grouping procedures account for any differences in achievement or in non-cognitive factors that occur between children in streamed and non-streamed schools. On the basis of this, J. Barker-Lunn (1970) has argued the importance of teachers' attitudes on methods of work. She claimed that one explanation for the inconsistent findings of research experiments was that different teachers responded differently to the form of organisation in the school. Some teachers believed in the system streamed or unstreamed; they used suitable methods and their pupils gained; other teachers could not accept the system or used inappropriate methods and their pupils did relatively badly. When the results obtained were averaged, little overall difference between the various forms of grouping was obtained.

Barker-Lunn concluded that in examining non-streamed schools, it was essential to take into account both the teaching methods adopted and the attitudes held by the teachers. The more traditional means of assessing academic achievements might be unsuitable for measuring the achievements of non-streamed schools, which after all aimed to do different things. As far as academic performance was concerned, this would appear to be unaffected by the kind of school organisation adopted. Progress seemed to be more a matter of the effectiveness of the individual teacher. However, minority groups in streamed schools were affected, particularly children in the overlap zone between streams: whereas those in a higher stream gained academically, those in a lower stream deteriorated. This finding was also emphasised by Douglas (1964). All recent studies, in emphasising the importance of the teacher, are generally agreed that non-streaming makes considerably greater demands on teachers in terms of planning and organisation.

It is important to realise in this situation of research confusion that the question of selection has important political consequences: streaming becomes linked with disadvantage. This is not completely inexplicable, for streaming processes produce 'disadvantaged' groups within a school by the formation of 'lower' streams. This fact was illustrated very clearly when, in 1967 in Washington DC, negro civic leaders brought a lawsuit on behalf of both negro and poor white children in that city. The court was asked to require by law an equal distribution to all city schools of funds, teachers and equipment. The lawsuit also asked for an injunction against the practice of streaming in city schools, on the grounds that grouping by ability worked to the disadvantage of negro and poor white children who, because of social and economic conditions outside school, often found themselves confined to bottom streams throughout their school life. The arguments were much the same as those already presented in Britain by those who have shown that streaming in British schools discriminates against the working class child.

A fact of very great importance was that the American Circuit Court of Appeals ruled against streaming, and grouping by ability is now virtually forbidden in Washington's schools. Most American schools are unstreamed anyway and always have been; allocation to classrooms has traditionally been by age alone. Streaming is practised by only 28 per cent of American primary schools and only 34 per cent of junior high schools. The implications of the court ruling could well have further effects on the practice of streaming in the United States.

It is necessary to recognise, therefore, that decisions about so fundamental an issue have political overtones and implications, particularly where it is a question of widening educational opportunity; the clarion calls, of egalitarianism on the one hand and of academic excellence on the other, will continue to be sounded. This is why it is important to attempt to separate educational selection from the wider issue of social or occupational selection. For the education system to abandon its function as an agency of social or occupational selection (by which pupils should gain the socio-economic rewards of a professional occupation and of high social position) would imply fundamental changes in the structure of society (see Chapter 7). This is rather different from the question of whether selection is important to the educational process itself. In other words, is streaming justified on educational grounds?

Even with this limited frame of reference, the UNESCO conference held at Hamburg in 1964 made it clear that most of the research on this question remained inconclusive. There are very real difficulties in assessing the effects of non-streaming, probably the most important being the criteria by which the change is evaluated. The abolition of streaming means the replacement and substitution of different educational aims and functions. If the research in this field shows anything, it appears to indicate that streamed schools have a slight advantage in teaching traditional subjects (mechanical and problem arithmetic and English). But streamed and non-streamed schools embody different educational philosophies. The former concentrates on more conventional lessons and applies examination-type standards to measure educational achievement. The latter places 'more emphasis on self-expression, learning by discovery and practical experience' (*Plowden Report*, 1967, vol. 2, pp. 572-3) and it is claimed that tests of educational achievement in this case require different instruments only now being developed.

Both pro- and anti-streamers want to achieve that method of school organisation which provides the environment best suited to encourage progress towards educational functions and purposes. The main difficulty is that each group holds different views about such educational functions and purposes. When this is further complicated by political considerations and the fact that streaming in education cannot be separated from social or occupational selection, any compromise is likely to be seen as unsatisfactory. The efficiency and effectiveness of streaming in education is dependent on the development by educationalists and psychologists of complex professional skills and techniques. But the question of to stream or not constitutes a dilemma only resolved by clarifying our educational ideals and understanding the relationship between these ideals and actual educational structures and institutions.

Comprehensive or selective secondary education

The problem of the most appropriate structure for secondary education involves further consideration of the question of selection as a technique for promoting educational and social goals, this time treating the schools themselves as the organisational unit. How do we draw the boundary line between the work done by one school and the work done by another? The alternatives seem to be: (1) to divide geographically and physically according to local residence patterns, in which case the school is a local school, comprehensive and all-inclusive in its teaching function. The idea that a comprehensive school must necessarily be a 'local' school has been abandoned since these frequently resulted in 'class' or 'ghetto' schools. A balanced social mix is a policy now frequently pursued for comprehensive schools. (2) The second alternative is to allow for some specialisation of the teaching and learning functions by distributing children between various schools according to their abilities, such that the tasks or goals which it is generally agreed the schools set themselves are specialised and differentiated.

There seems to be general agreement that a certain 'phase' of education, that known as 'primary', comes to an end at the age of about ten or eleven. Thereafter, a rather more specialised form of education begins, continuing until the individual either leaves school at sixteen, or goes on to enter higher education at eighteen plus, or continues into further education at sixteen plus, either full-time or part-time. This middle stage of education, known as the secondary stage, has proved to be the most controversial in terms of the school structure and nature of the curriculum most appropriate to it. Probably the most disputed issue is the question of selection at the point of change from primary to secondary and the distribution of children according to their abilities into different types of school, specialising on rather different educational objectives. As stated above, the alternatives appear to be: on the one hand some sort of 'common' secondary school, ideally unstreamed and with a common curriculum, catering for all levels of ability up to the point of specialisation for higher education; this is the so-called 'comprehensive' secondary school principle. On the other hand, the alternative is the selection of children according to their abilities at the point of entry to secondary education, on some criteria which might include an English and Arithmetic test, an IQ test, teachers' and headmasters' reports, parents' and child's wishes, etc. The children are then distributed between different types of school: to the English Grammar School (French Lycée, German Gymnasium) go the children of high ability and with ambitions to undertake a higher education; in such selective schools, teaching tends to be subject-centred and high academic standards are valued. For the children who do not meet the high ability requirements of such schools, the alternatives are some sort of technical school, where one exists, with a more practical bent and approach to subjects, often connected with the world of work, or a secondary modern school or central school for the rest to continue their general education up to school leaving age. This is a selective secondary school system incorporating a tripartite or bipartite structure.

The problem of the organisation of secondary education is by no means peculiar to Britain, although Britain has a long tradition of high status grammar schools which make any suggestion of change in the structure very controversial. In Britain, while we are still considering several possible alternatives, a number of countries have made changes. Sweden has decided that little or no selection or differentiation should take place in school before the age of sixteen. The French have likewise arrived at a 'common school' but only for the eleven to fifteen age group. In the United States, the common school principle has always been in operation. Nine years of school attendance are required and this usually includes six elementary grades and three junior high school grades. Students can then pass, without examination, into the senior high school where most pupils remain until graduation. In the senior high school the pupil is entirely free in his choice of subjects. Mostly, subjects will be grouped into systematic courses usually divided into: classical, foreign languages, household, commercial, technical, social sciences, science, maths, history, etc. All courses and subjects are equivalent and the same amount of credits are required for high school graduation in Latin or domestic science, although children intending to go on to higher education will select academic courses.

In most countries, developed and developing, the past twenty years have seen pressures for change towards some sort of comprehensive secondary school organisation; pressures which come largely from progressives who criticise subject-centred, academic traditions and would emphasise education centred on the child. Frank Bowles (1963) classified school systems at the beginning of the 1960-70 decade according to the type of separation that follows primary education. Bowles studied ninety-three countries and concluded that evolution towards a two-tier structure and away from a two-track structure was marked.

The situation in England is, as in other countries with a history of selective secondary education, a matter of dispute. Many educationalists argue for the abolition of the eleven plus examination and the tripartite or bipartite system of secondary education, and for the universal substitution of comprehensive education as more socially just, economically viable and educationally defensible. Other educationalists argue for the retention of selective secondary education especially in areas where a grammar school exists with long traditions of academic excellence; this would be in the interests of children of all abilities and especially the really bright children; experiments in comprehensive secondary education should be restricted to widespread rural populations where they are more appropriate.

Agreement with, or opposition to, selection in secondary education is consistent with views on the nature of human intelligence, perceptions of the knowledge-ideal and conceptions of the education process. Idealists will favour selective secondary education; progressives advocate a comprehensive secondary school system. In England, the contemporary dispute had its origins in the 1944 Education Act which failed to specify any particular kind of secondary organisation but left the decision open to local authorities to make arrangements appropriate to their areas, although hope was expressed that some authorities would experiment with comprehensive education. A few local education authorities (London, Coventry, Bristol and the West Riding of Yorkshire) were able to press for the introduction of comprehensive education from the start. Most local authorities opted for a tripartite or bipartite secondary school system when they reorganised their elementary schools. A large number of authorities did not set up technical schools. Two-tier structures, grammar and secondary modern, were common. This type of organisation fitted most readily with existing arrangements: the grammar school remained, as before, and the elementary school became the secondary modern school.

However, throughout the 1950s there was a definite shift in public opinion. Discontent with the eleven plus examination increased and a number of local authorities, particularly county authorities, reorganised their secondary schools along comprehensive lines. (Of special note was the Leicestershire Plan, with its two tiers, which was designed to make best use of existing staff, buildings and equipment.) By the early 1960s, three-quarters of local authorities either had, or were planning to have, at least one comprehensive school. The next development came in 1965 when the Department of Education, under the instructions of the new

Labour Government, issued Circular 10/65, 'requesting' local education authorities to submit plans for comprehensive schemes for their areas; this circular was sent out with a certain amount of confidence that there had already been a move in public opinion in favour of comprehensive education in the country.

The request met with a certain amount of success; by 1970 over three-quarters (129 out of 163) of local education authorities had implemented comprehensive schemes or had them approved. When the circular was sent out, 8 per cent of children were in comprehensives; in 1970 there were 26 per cent. In 1965, there were 262 comprehensives; in 1970, 1,200. However, looked at from the other point of view, 74 per cent of the children in local authority secondary schools still went to grammar, technical or secondary modern schools in 1970. The percentage of children who had to sit some form of eleven plus was higher since all but twenty-six of the local education authorities continued to select pupils for one or other type of secondary education. (Statistics from the 1970 survey of the Comprehensive Schools Committee, 1969. Reported in *New Society* 12 February 1970.)

But even where comprehensives were in operation, they came in various forms: all-through schools were for eleven to sixteen or eleven to eighteen year olds; two-tier schools were for eleven to thirteen or eleven to fourteen followed by thirteen to eighteen or fourteen to eighteen schools; sixth form colleges took in pupils at sixteen; middle schools straddled the eleven plus division between primary and secondary education and ran from eight to twelve years or from nine to thirteen. Comprehensives were intended to be non-selective and for all the children in a district. However, the Department of Education, in considering plans submitted to it by local authorities, had considered merely the minimum requirements in giving its approval: schools were supposed to be non-selective and to provide a range of post-O level courses.

The question of what form the secondary school organisation should take was genuinely the choice of the local authority and there were several possible alternatives. Further, there was wide variety within these alternatives, depending on geographical factors and the size of the schools. Some authorities gave high priority to the need for social mix, zoning their schools to get a predetermined catchment to try to overcome the 'ghetto' criticism of local comprehensives. Others tried to ensure that no school was totally without bright children and 'banded' accordingly. When 'banding' is applied, levels of ability are determined by anonymous testing and each school is rationed on numbers of children from each ability grouping. Inner London Education Authority and Haringey have now introduced a banding system. Some authorities maintained a hidden form of selection. Benn and Simon (1970) give the following examples: schools abolish selection at eleven, but in two-tier systems; children were allowed to transfer to a school with A level courses only if they were likely to stay on for A levels. Alternately, there might be a sixth form which was purely academic. Again, there could be eleven to sixteen schools existing alongside eleven to eighteen schools and the latter, becoming the local sixth form centres, might again be purely academic. Even further than this, it was the headmaster's decision in the school itself which determined to what extent the school operated a streaming system and divided children by abilities within year groups or a 'setting' system, dividing children by ability within subject groups.

Even with such a range of alternatives (or perhaps because of it) the comprehensive movement ran into difficulties. Twenty-two local authorities either refused to submit comprehensive plans or had them rejected. Birmingham, one of the biggest authorities in the country, refused to submit plans. But further than this, very few authorities had gone totally comprehensive. Leicestershire was probably the only totally comprehensive authority of any size. At present, there is a mixed system in operation with as many grammar schools as there are comprehensives: nearly 900 fully maintained county grammar schools and about 180 of the 'voluntary-aided' type (Benn and Simon, 1970). In addition, there are 179 direct grant schools, over which a local authority has no effective control. To add to the confusion, a white paper published by the Conservative Party in 1958 ('Secondary Education for all—a new drive') recommended that secondary modern schools be encouraged to develop post-O level courses in addition to the grammar schools. During the 1960s, the secondary modern schools began to develop their GCE courses. The attempt to organise a curriculum undirected by examination criteria in the secondary modern schools seemed doomed to failure as a result of parental and pupil pressure to be permitted to take part in the attempt to achieve nationally recognised qualifications. The setting up of the Certificate of Secondary Education (CSE) examinations in 1965 marked a compromise in this respect. Although intended as a nationally recognised educational qualification, by presenting teachers with the opportunities to set papers and mark candidates, it freed both teacher and pupil to follow interests and schemes that were impossible for teacher and pupil following a highly structured GCE course.

One of the main consequences of this diversity of structure and organisation of secondary education was a polarisation of discontent concerning perceived future developments. Many progressives were increasingly critical of the slow progress of real comprehensivisation; many idealists condemned the challenges to the traditions of the grammar school and the watering down of know-ledge-ideals. In the face of mounting criticism, the Labour Government presented an Education Bill before Parliament in 1970. The bill had three clauses:

(i) local education authorities were to have regard to the need to secure that secondary education was provided in non-selective schools, though sixth forms and sixth form colleges could select;

(ii) the Secretary of State for Education could require local authorities to submit one or more plans for going comprehensive and he could require them to revise plans;

(iii) plans might anyway be revised after a five-year period.

This bill was in fact rejected in committee as a result of the absence of a number of the Labour members and returned to the House. Soon after, in June 1970, the Labour Government was defeated in a general election and a Conservative Government returned to power. One of the first actions of the new Secretary of State for Education in the Conservative Government, Mrs Margaret Thatcher, was to withdraw the original Circular 10/65 to local authorities. In future, according to Circular 10/70, local authorities were to determine their secondary education policies with regard primarily to local area needs.

It is necessary to be aware, therefore, of the way in which attitudes towards the comprehensive issue, as attitudes towards the selection question in general, have changed over the past twenty years. As has been stated earlier (see Chapter 4), the early supporters of the comprehensive principle looked to the new schools to overcome class barriers and inequalities. Later supporters stressed efficiency and a fuller use of the nation's supplies of potential talent. It was the efficiency rather than the equality argument that caught the public imagination. Certainly the eleven plus examination had become highly unpopular but as was shown by the reception of the Labour Government's proposed legislation, this was definitely not a mandate for the abolition of the grammar school. *New Society* (October 1967), publishing the results of an opinion poll, claimed that although 52 per cent of the population said they were in favour of comprehensive schooling (29 per cent did not know), in another question 46 per cent chose grammar schooling for their own child and only 16 per cent comprehensive. In a further question, 76 per cent wanted to retain grammar school-ing and only 15 per cent were against it. Obviously this was not a vote for comprehensives so much as a massive vote against the secondary modern school.

Idealists, critical of the universal implementation of comprehensive schooling, give various reasons for their opinions. For many this was a point of principle in that the 'destruction' of the grammar school would mean the end of centuries of academic traditions of excellence. Often comprehensives were condemned as being positively harmful to precisely the working class children they were designed to help, in that bright working class children could best succeed by going to grammar schools. The one-standard issue is important here. Certainly if education requires 'middle class' attitudes and values, then the earlier they are 'taught', the better. This matter is never adequately dealt with by those who condemn the grammar school for being a middle class institution. However, for many critics of comprehensive education, the comprehensive question was not so much one of principle as one of actual practice. Examples of chaos resulting from reorganisation were very numerous and simply to relabel a secondary modern school in a run-down slum area as a comprehensive school solved nothing. Money was needed in very large amounts for the comprehensive principle to have a chance of proving itself, but the money was not forthcoming. Further than this, many idealists saw dangers in the wholesale change to comprehensive education in what many saw as 'the present anti-intellectual climate'. Comprehensive schools did not automatically mean a decline in academic standards, but in the contemporary 'anti-cultural' culture, where there was considerable hostility to intellectual disciplines, they did pose a very real threat to those standards and disciplines.

A stalemate exists at the present time over the question of whether comprehensives can coexist with grammar and direct grant schools. Many progressives say they cannot and in conceptual terms they are quite right since by definition a comprehensive school must be all-inclusive. Many idealists say they can and though in principle they are wrong, the present compromise policy says otherwise. If comprehensives coexist with a full system of selection and grammar schools then the result is obviously no change at all. But, as many idealists argue, if one or two grammar schools were to remain in an otherwise fully comprehensive system, the results would be far less damaging educationally even though the comprehensive 'principle' had been breached.

The clash of principle between the progressives and the idealists on the comprehensive problem is clear enough. Idealists claim that the process of education itself would be threatened by such a far-reaching structural change. Progressives advance both social and academic arguments in favour of such a change: they claim that it is not necessary to choose between equality and preserving quality, for the comprehensive school would also raise general levels of attainment. Both sides have tried to advance their arguments by empirical research and the manipulation of statistical evidence. The sorts of arguments advanced fall into two categories: firstly, the comparison of achievements in different types of school, usually by comparing success rate in GCE O and A level examinations; secondly, a comparison between comprehensive and tripartite school children concerning the non-cognitive or social aspects of education.

Comparing success rates in GCE examinations between comprehensive and tripartite schools (Ford, 1969), Robin Pedley (1963) noted that in spite of the fact that many of these schools had been 'creamed' by local grammar schools, some 14 per cent of his sample had gained five or more O level passes. This compared with a national figure of about 10 per cent for tripartite schools.

But, as Robin Davis has pointed out (1967), Pedley's claim was based on figures up to 1962, that is, before secondary modern schools had started to enter candidates for GCE examinations on a large scale. The 1965 results presented a different picture. Davis compared the O level passes of children in London comprehensives with those of secondary modern children and no important differences emerged. The proportion of O level passes was higher in the comprehensives in some subjects but lower in others. In other words, even if the argument that most of the present comprehensives were 'creamed' of their best pupils is accepted and their results are compared only with the results of secondary modern schools, the comprehensives do not appear to be producing better results.

However, as Ford shows, Davis's analysis can itself be criticised. The comparative success rates of examination candidates are only partly a function of the relative quality of the candidates. A high rate of examination success in one school might be a reflection of a very effective school organisation and teaching programme; in another school, however, the same 'success' rate (i.e. defined as numbers gaining five or more O levels) might merely reflect a highly restrictive policy towards examination entrants. Ford concludes that Davis has not shown that the comprehensives are doing no better than secondary modern schools in public examinations because the two schools are not comparable. The comprehensive schools might be entering as many children as possible for GCE examinations in order to maximise the absolute number of GCE results obtained. In fact, there is some evidence that the comprehensives are entering more children in an attempt to increase the absolute numbers of qualifications gained. A reanalysis of Pedley's figures (in *Observer*, January 1965; see also Douglas Young and Walter Brandis, 1967) has shown that, for every 100 children entered for some O levels by all local education authorities, the fully comprehensive schools entered 121 candidates, while the creamed comprehensives entered 172 candidates. It could be argued, further, that those secondary modern schools which enter most pupils for GCE examinations are most likely to be schools with the largest proportion of middle class pupils; therefore the comprehensive and secondary modern school populations are not comparable.

The evidence of examination results is inconclusive at present, therefore. In order for a valid comparison between comprehensive and tripartite schools to be made, it would be necessary to hold constant IQ and social class of pupils, teaching ability as well as the examination policies of the schools. To quote Ford:

> Does the working class comprehensive school pupil of average intelligence have a better chance of obtaining GCE qualifications than the similar child in a secondary modern school? Does the 'bright' child stand as good a chance of success if he attends the comprehensive as if he goes to the grammar school? In short, does comprehensive education produce more talented performances in public examinations? At present, we simply do not know.

However, achievement or success rates in public examinations are not the only criteria for assessing the relative advantages of comprehensive over selective secondary schooling (or vice versa). Ford examines five hypotheses, two referring to 'academic' and three referring to 'social' arguments that comprehensive education would constitute a major step towards the creation of a 'fairer society'. The five hypotheses are:

(i) that early selection prevents the fullest development of talent;

(ii) that early selection inhibits equality of educational opportunity for those with equal talent;

(iii) that type of school determines occupational horizons;

(iv) that friendship groups are affected by education, occupation and class factors;

(v) that perceptions of stratification are related to educational experience.

No evidence is found to support any of the hypotheses and the conclusion is reached that the theory itself must be faulty.

Obviously, such a conclusion is only acceptable if we are willing to accept the working definitions and indices that are employed, and the methods used, to test the hypotheses, and this need not be the case. We must conclude, however, that at the present time factual evidence is inconclusive. Indeed, it is unrealistic to demand such factual evidence. Instead, we must clarify what the alternatives are, what are the likely consequences of each alternative, who makes the choices and the priority decisions and how these decisions are influenced. It is an important fact that the government's role is limited in the making of these major decisions concerning secondary school organisation; this is true under both Labour and Conservative governments. The government specifies needs, and gets the local education authority to provide for them. But the government does not take the initiative in actually *doing* anything in education. The Labour Government might have changed all this, if it had been really determined to turn the country comprehensive. But even their proposed Education Bill was concerned with plans and not implementation and went no way towards changing the balance between central government and the local education authorities. Obviously, there are some things such as school leaving age and a number of minimum specifications which must be settled by the government. At the other extreme, it would clearly be undesirable for a government to specify curriculum, textbooks and teaching techniques in any detail. But in between, there is a wide area where it is more difficult to be dogmatic about the right division of responsibilities, and school structure and organisation is clearly an important problem in this area.

However, a government must have some attitude on the comprehensive issue. Other considerations apart, the Department of Education has to approve all school building programmes and must apply some criteria in accepting and rejecting schemes. It could be argued that Mrs Thatcher, by not openly stating what her priorities will be, or by leaving them vague, will be increasing the central government's control. Since she will be judging each case on how it affects the interested parties, or how they are able to convince her that it affects them, rather than according to precedents built up (for example, following the Labour Circular 10/65) of the educational viability of a particular pattern, she is giving herself more power in making decisions.

Had the Labour Party been returned to office in 1970, presumably a different principle would have been embodied in legislation : local authorities would have been compelled to adopt a comprehensive system, but would have been able to decide which of the many variations to implement. The difficulties in enforcing this principle are those inherent in the whole notion of compulsion, and the uproar that would have accompanied any challenge to local authority freedom, especially if the challenge was not backed by a large proportion of vocal public opinion. It is difficult to decide what 'democracy' means in such circumstances. Does it mean preserving local freedom of choice or impelling the will of the central government for the supposed 'good' of the national majority? There are many criticisms made of the sort of people who run local government and of the peculiarities of a system where the amateur gives orders to the professional. Richard Crossman, writing his first editorial in *New Statesman*, condemned 'the butchers and bakers, without any serious interest in education'. On the other hand, there are the supporters of the system who have an almost mystical belief in the virtue of local democracy in spite of the depressing evidence about its actual performance. If we are convinced of the value of local democracy, this often means accepting great disparities in standards of educational provision, and therefore of opportunities, between local authority areas. But, equally problematical, is to decide on increasing the amount of central direction when this also means to increase dependence on the managerial competence of a huge civil service. Any compromise decision inevitably means that the fine principles of both progressives and idealists will become blurred in practice.

In the next section, we consider the wider implications of divergence and dispute among educationalists. The consequences of selection in education for other social institutions, the question of choice in education and the alternative models for the administration of the education system also pose dilemmas. Again there is patterning between the alternatives such that educational philosophies are consistent with, and predictable from, attitudes to the market economy, to the management of knowledge and the desirable relationship between education, man and society.

Part Two

Education and society

6

The organisation of education: the influence of economic models

As societies become industrialized, the education system becomes increasingly important. Education is inextricably bound up with economics, the economy financing education and education producing the manpower recruits for the economy. On a wider level of generalisation, if education is seen as a socialising institution responsible for passing on the values and culture of the society to each new generation, then education makes substantial contributions to the maintenance of society itself. In pre-industrial societies, the education of the child was simply his general upbringing and training in essential attitudes, practices and skills. As societies industrialised, education became a separate institution in its own right with its own values, goals and techniques.

Societies obviously differ from one another in many ways and in many respects. Yet, virtually since the beginnings of their discipline, sociologists have differentiated within this endless diversity between two broad types of society. In the first, organisation was based on uniformity and was obtained primarily by force. In the second, differences, particularly in the division of labour, were basic to the organisation of society and harmony was dependent on freely made agreements. In the eighteenth century Saint Simon distinguished between military and industrial forms of society. The military form, which was based on nationalism and maintained by armed force, was being replaced at that time by a form of society dependent on cooperation between employers, workers and traders. Émile Durkheim contrasted societies held together by mechanical solidarity and those held together by organic solidarity. Sir Henry Maine distinguished between a society based on status and one based on contract. Herbert Spencer labelled the two types militant and industrial. In militant forms of society people were organised as a nation; rank and chains of command were specified and industry was subordinated to the government's requirements. By contrast, in industrial types of society, free exchange was a central economic feature, cooperation was secured by voluntary means and the keeping of agreements was a basic moral requirement. Spencer's view of industrial society was largely a result of his reaction against mercantilism, whereby governments interfered more and more with economic affairs. 'Mercantilism' represented a system under which the government controlled the manufacture and pricing of goods and the development of industry and trade in order to secure a favourable balance of trade for the country. Spencer deplored this situation and advocated instead a sort of spontaneously regulated society in which goods were allowed to be freely produced and exchanged. The term 'laissez-faire' began to be used to represent a system with a spontaneous and 'natural' industrial and commercial system, where market principles of supply and demand and pricing mechanisms were allowed free play and where the government did not interfere in economic affairs. In time, the term 'laissez-faire' came to be used much more generally to denote a system where the government did not intervene, or intervened as little as possible, in any situation, economic, legal, social or educational. Rather, the operation of market forces, competition and the profit motive became guiding principles.

'Laissez-faire' was the political principle governing the early development of the education system. Demands for education were met first by private initiative, by setting up independently financed and organised schools and universities. Then, as the crucial importance of education was recognised, this was followed by increasing state intervention and control. Dilemmas remain, however, concerning the relevance and significance to education of market principles and economic criteria of efficiency. It is intended to show how market principles continue to influence our conceptions of an effective education system. This is so in spite of recurrent assertions that educational institutions cannot be judged by such criteria and that alternative structures and organisations can only be contrasted and compared according to 'educational' criteria. First, however, it is necessary to examine the history and development of the market principle, together with the history of the centralisation of control and direction in education.

The growth of state control and direction of education

Traditionally, education was controlled by the church. For centuries the educational system consisted of a set of independently financed schools and universities dominated by religious stipulations and precepts. In this country, the idea of state intervention or central administrative machinery developed very slowly. The belief in laissez-faire was strong and the wisdom of state intervention was hotly disputed. The state avoided intervention because of the confrontation with the church that this would have entailed. Before the Elementary Education Act of 1870, the government limited its share in educational provision to making small subsidies to voluntary religious bodies who provided and managed church elementary schools. In 1870, the local authorities were empowered to provide board schools at the elementary level. These were to work alongside the voluntary schools belonging to the various religious bodies and were intended primarily to fill the gaps left by them. Since then, this dual system has been modified and developed but it is still in operation (Lester Smith, 1965). The system was continued, although reshaped, by the 1944 Education Act. Voluntary schools were to receive more state aid and in return accept more state control. In 1959, parliament confirmed the system when another Education Act increased the voluntary school building grant from 50 to 75 per cent and again in 1966 when a further increase to 80 per cent was announced.

Religion is not now the explosive issue that it was once in education. Divisions over educational issues today are figuring more and more prominently in party politics. The first time this happened was during the passage of the 1902 Education Act which intended to transfer the local government of education from the school boards to the newly created local education authorities and also to buttress the finances of the voluntary schools. Since then, state interference and control over education have increased, and the system of party politics has ensured that at least on some issues there are opportunities for public consideration of opposing opinions. Another reason why education comes so much into politics today is that, with increasing state control and finance, the education service has to compete with other essential government services for the allocation of resources in the government's programme. Finally, reasonably comparable standards of educational provision throughout the country cannot be achieved unless there is central direction to encourage uniform standards in all areas.

The laissez-faire situation in education gradually declined. It was replaced by a two-tier system of control, central direction and local implementation. The basis of educational administration today rests on the relationship between the central government's Department of Education and Science (formerly the Ministry of Education) and the local education authorities of local government. Under laissez-faire conditions, the school structure had consisted of a number of public or independent schools, usually boarding their pupils, and self-financing out of fees, and a growing number of voluntary schools financed by religious bodies and subject to their control. Increasingly since 1870 the state has provided new schools and taken over voluntary schools such that a state school structure, in cooperation with the church and local authorities, now exists over the whole country and provides 'free' (although financed by taxation and rates) education in primary, secondary and further education sectors. A public or independent school system continues alongside the state system. In the 1920s direct grant schools opted to receive their grants direct from the Board of Education rather than indirectly from the local authorities. They have continued in this anomalous position, neither wholly of the state nor completely independent.

Within the state system, the law carefully provides for power to be distributed and puts stress on 'national policy', which is decided by the minister, and 'effective execution', which is to be undertaken by the local authority. In the 1899 Education Act provision was made for a central Board of Education with a President whose duties were specified as the superintendence of matters relating to education. The role of the Minister of Education, as defined by the 1944 Education Act, is very different. As laid down in the provisions of the Act, his powers are very wide-ranging. He has a general obligation to present to parliament any rules that he proposes to enforce. But, subject only to this limitation, he has the power to overrule any local education authority or school governors within the state system if they act contrary to his purpose. He sets out his requirements by means of statutory rules, orders, regulations and circulars. These powers enable him to deal with priorities as he sees them, to insist on minimum standards and even out differences in the quality of education between local areas, and to see that there is regional or national provision for particular needs. (The extent of the power of the Minister of Education and the limits on his authority are discussed in Kogan, 1971.)

The Robbins Report recommended the appointment of two ministers, one to be responsible for universities and other autonomous yet state-supported institutions, and the other to have the same responsibilities that the minister has at present. However, current policy emphasised the unity and coordination of government departments and so this recommendation was rejected. In 1964, the Ministry of Education became the Department of Education and Science with a Secretary of State at its head. The Secretary appoints two Ministers of State under him, one to be responsible for the schools of England and Wales, the other for institutions of university status. Since 1964 the University Grants Committee has been responsible to the Secretary of State for Education and Science rather than receiving its grant direct from the Treasury.

The Secretary is required by law to appoint two Central Advisory Councils (one for England, one for Wales) to advise him on problems of educational theory and practice. The Crowther, Newsom and Plowden Reports are examples of recent research done by the Central Advisory Councils on the Government's behalf. Apart from this, the Secretary is assisted and advised by the Department of Education and Science. The Department has a staff of about 3000 of whom 80 belong to the administrative grade (Lester Smith, 1965). In addition, there are professional civil servants within the Department such as lawyers, architects, statisticians and inspectors (HMIs).

The second tier of the administrative structure consists of the local authorities, in particular the local education authorities, with their responsibilities for execution of central government policy. This system of government has been criticised many times; many of the criticisms stem from the occupational make-up of many councils where it has been found that retired people and housewives predominate. Active membership in an Education Committee requires almost full-time service and this makes it impossible for many people who are concerned with education, teachers in particular, to serve. There is provision for education committees to coopt members with experience in education and knowledge of schools, but these will be in an advisory capacity only. The future of the present local authority system is under much discussion today with the publication of the Maud Report in 1969 and the Bill now before Parliament containing proposals issued by Peter Walker in 1971. The Maud Report recommended the setting up of fifty-eight large unitary authorities (cities and boroughs) with extensive powers and responsibilities. The local urban and rural districts were to advise only. The Bill now before Parliament proposes to retain a two-tier structure of (i) metropolitan and county councils with responsibility for most functions, and (ii) local district councils with limited responsibility in which housing is included. Many people remain convinced of the need for strong local authorities to act as a balancing mechanism against the powers of the central government. Other people would prefer to see education administered locally or regionally by an ad hoc body (i.e. the setting up of education boards like the school boards created in 1870) which would operate like the regional hospital boards.

The present two-tier system of educational administration,

99

whereby a considerable amount of freedom is allowed to the local authorities in the carrying out of central government directives, has important consequences. Perhaps the most conspicuous are the differences in the percentages of students entering higher education from the schools of different local education authorities. In 1966, the percentages ranged from 24·9 per cent in Cardiganshire to 5·1 per cent in the Isle of Ely for the counties and from 17·9 per cent in Oxford to 1·7 per cent in West Ham for the county boroughs. The Robbins Report indicates that in areas where more than 23 per cent of pupils went to grammar school, 11 per cent of the age group entered higher education. In areas where grammar school entry was low, 18 per cent of the age group or under, only 7·5 per cent entered higher education.

Similarly average class size varied between local authority areas and class size can be seen as an important variable influencing the percentages of students entering higher education. In areas where primary school classes contained on average thirty-seven pupils or more, only 7·7 per cent of the age group entered higher education compared with 11·4 per cent in areas where average class size was thirty-two or fewer. In secondary schools, in areas where classes had less than twenty per teacher, 11·3 per cent of the age group went on to higher education compared with 6·9 per cent where classes had twenty-three or more pupils. A study done by S. John Eggleston in seven Midland local education authorities showed widespread differences in provision of selective and non-selective secondary education and, particularly, differences in the provision of extended courses and other opportunities for pupils to stay on after the minimum school leaving age. (Taylor, 1971, confirms these findings.) It is quite clear, therefore, that the educational opportunities for young people are affected by the administrative arrangements of the local authority in which they happen to be educated.

With the finance of education, the trend has again been one of increasing state intervention. Until the Fisher Act of 1918, government finance amounted to a haphazard system of small subsidies to voluntary bodies and to local authorities. With the passing of the Fisher Act, a percentage grant system was introduced whereby the central government contributed about 60 per cent of educational expenditure and the local authorities, from their rates, contributed about 40 per cent. The proportion of costs met by the central government has tended to increase (Vaizey, 1958; Vaizey and Sheehan, 1968). Following the Local Government Act of 1958, the percentage grant system was abolished. Instead, education was included among other services covered by a general grant paid to the local authorities. Thus, the government pays a block general grant to local authorities and places on them the responsibility of deciding how much to pay in respect of each local government service. Their freedom to decide how much to spend on education is limited, however, for there are numerous important statutory and other requirements which a local authority is obliged to fulfil.

Many of the important questions that arise when the finance of education and the importance of strong central direction are under discussion relate to the willingness of taxpayers to support education as a social service compared with their willingness to support it as an item of personal consumption (Hall and Lauwerys in Lauwerys, 1969). It seems likely that if education is financed as a social service by money from central government funds, then a larger proportion of the gross national product will be spent on education than where the money is raised locally and education is regarded as an item of personal consumption. However, this cannot automatically be assumed and Lauwerys suggests that the system of educational administration in the United States of America would seem to disprove this association. If education is regarded as a consumer item, and it is of a type that the public appreciate, then local taxation could bring in more money than central government finance. Such an arrangement also has a number of other advantages. Education becomes comparatively free from hard and fast traditional educational norms; it is more flexible and more easily modified towards consumer demand. At the present time, our approach to educational administration and finance tends to confuse the two principles, however (Hall and Lauwerys):

> If education is to be regarded as a consumer item it has to be responsive to consumer demand. Decentralised control makes this possible. If, on the other hand, education is to be seen as a social service, central government may then be expected to provide most of the funds. It can explain its policy in terms of social usefulness and respond to suggestions for improving this usefulness. It is worth repeating that many administrations fail to distinguish between a social service and a consumer item. This justification allows them to administer the service as though it were a consumer item, but with 'experts' to decide what the consumer wants.

Together with increased state intervention in control and administration of the educational system has gone a change in attitudes towards the way education should be supported and the perceived relationship between education and the society. When a laissez-faire philosophy was prevalent in society and the provision of schools was left to individual initiative, education, particularly at higher levels, was seen as a consumer item and as something intended for a small and select group. The content of education was determined by what the consumers, the parents, demanded. The sort of education that was given was concerned with character-building and with preparing an elite for administrative and leader-ship roles. Schools were set up as commercial enterprises offering a desirable commodity, education, to those who were able to pay. Those with sufficient wealth could choose the type of education and school that they desired and a market proposition was trans-acted.

When the churches began to set up their own voluntary schools, the kind of education that was given in such schools was of a different kind. Only the kinds of knowledge and skill that were considered relevant and necessary to a humble, obedient, Christian life were taught in such schools. The content of the education for the masses was determined by what those in authority per-ceived such children to require. Education was, consciously or un-consciously, being used as an agent of socialisation and an instru-ment of economic and social control. But the market was in decline as the guiding principle; laissez-faire was no longer the dominant government philosophy, particularly with respect to education. As state intervention grew, education came to be seen increasingly as a basic human right. The Bill of Human Rights drawn up by the United Nations assumes that every human being has a right to be educated just as he has an inalienable right to pursue life, liberty and happiness. In the advanced nations this has resulted in education being regarded as an essential social service. Education has been organised and financed by central governments alongside their other social services, health and welfare provisions. Social service principles of equality and social justice have influenced the content of education.

In recent years, however, there has been a revival of interest in an economic model for the education system, as when efficiency replaces social justice as the criterion for judging the effectiveness of various methods of educational organisation and administration. It is widely held that, in advanced industrial countries, a society cannot afford less education than the maximum it is able to finance. Examples are given of drastic shortages of technically competent manpower. Economies are seen to be dependent on large-scale investments in education.

In so far as the production pattern of any economy is dependent on many factors (capital, raw materials, and its trained labour force), the relative importance of education for economic advance is difficult to assess. An important influence that education can exert on the economy is in developing and influencing consumer attitudes (Foster, 1965). Increasingly it is suggested that a correlation exists between investment in education and the growth of national income in a society. Also, it is certain that education will be a major limiting factor on the extent and success of attempts to introduce changes (such as mechanisation and automation) in the organisation of work. According to G. U. Papi (Vaizey and Robinson, 1966), education should make individuals more receptive to inventions and innovations. Education must promote the division of labour and the use of machinery; it must permit increasingly advantageous combinations of the factors of production; it must help to expedite the operating of any new technical discovery; and it must promote an extensive mobility of labour and of entrepreneurial ability. When educationalists speak vaguely of education for 'flexibility of mind' or 'mobility of thought' or 'breadth of vision', Professor Papi's suggestions are how the economist sees these applying to a developing technological and inventive society.

Interest has been shown in attempts to estimate the cost-benefit effects of educational expenditure and a 'human capital' approach to educational planning. The use of such terms indicates the perceived importance of economic models for the educational system.

One group of educationalists would go further and assert the appropriateness for the educational system, not only of economic models, but also of free market principles of competitive provision and consumer choice. Such views will be examined. Criticism of a return to free market principles is widespread but critics nevertheless acknowledge the importance of economic principles of rational organisation, of efficiency in the definition and pursuit of goals and of planning to eliminate wastage in the system.

The market principle and the educational system

The market principles of consumer choice and competitive supply are advocated in education for two main reasons. Firstly, the choice that is an essential element in the market situation is an important element of human freedom. The responsibility of choosing is essential for that freedom to continue. Secondly, competition in supply is the most efficient means of organisation since it enables production and distribution of services to be set against the needs and wants of consumers.

The responsibilities that choice places on the individual are, supposedly, an essential element in human freedom. It is argued that, through the price mechanism, parents (and children) can establish their own priorities of wants and needs since it is possible for 'want' and 'need' to be interpreted in different ways by those receiving and those making any distribution of services. By increasing state interference, we are at the same time allowing the state to decide what individuals need and want. This is to magnify all the disadvantages that monopolies have in hindering the free play of supply and demand in a market. To reassert the market principle involves a questioning of paternalistic assumptions and a giving back to individuals of greater opportunities for shaping and controlling their services. This means that in regard to such basic needs as education (health, housing, etc.) it is best for people to allocate their own resources as far as they can, with public provision (in purchasing power, if possible) in reserve for what they cannot afford. Ralph Harris and Arthur Seldon (1963, 1965, 1970) are interested in how far markets, with their advantages of competition between suppliers and choice for consumers, could play a larger part in all our services than governments at present allow for. Harris and Seldon have attempted to measure public preferences between taxes for state services and charges (financed by insurance) for private services by attaching price tags to alternatives. The financial arrangements for the new system would involve cash refunds and vouchers, together with a contribution from individuals which would be designed to cover the whole of school expenditure. E. G. West is one of the main advocates of this method of organisation for the education system. West (1965, 1967, 1968) argues that where education is provided as a social service, there will always be a convergence of educational policy in a two-party political system, and that attention will be diverted away from the deficiencies of the system. Talent will be maximised only where parents are given much more freedom of choice in education.

Furthermore, where market principles operate, there is no need to plan the educational system with the aim of increasing efficient operation. Indeed, planning can only interfere with the efficient operation of market principles. The 'hidden hand' of the market will ensure that the needs and wants of individuals are met since their demands will be reconciled automatically with the forces of supply through the pricing mechanism. In this case, planning and interference by central governments, beyond ensuring a basic minimum provision, are irrelevant and inappropriate. The market, through competition that arises from cash demand, is the most effective way of meeting individuals' needs and wants. State intervention can mean only inefficiency since nationalised industries, government departments and state welfare organisations all have to be organised in bureaucratic forms with directors, committees and chains of command and responsibility.

Critics of the free market principle, particularly in education and other social services, are concerned primarily with the injustices and inequalities that are seen to be the inevitable consequence of private choice in these areas. Brian Barry (1965) puts forward three arguments in favour of eliminating competition and private payments for services to meet basic needs. Firstly, a society which permits payment and choice in education and welfare will have, as a consequence, a number of hierarchically arranged subgroups in the population. Some will be privileged and others not, and there will be no shared experience or standards. Barry believes integration to be an important element in democracy. Secondly, inefficiency as well as injustice will result from such arrangements since wealth rather than ability will secure a powerful future position. Thirdly, in an integrated system, where the wealthy and powerful have to use the same services as the rest, they are more likely to be encouraged to improve the public provision and make them as good as possible.

H. B. Acton (1971) replies to these points in the following way:

> In a society where the free market has scope, the better-off
> tend to pioneer various types of consumption which are
> then made available to larger sections of the population. The
> same principle, I suggest, applies to welfare, especially to
> education where private schools have set standards and
> carried out experiments which the publicly provided schools
> have then made beneficial use of. As to Dr Barry's second
> argument, it seems to me that a free market economy is less
> prone to hierarchy than is the bureaucratic sort of society
> that socialism requires. As to the alleged 'divisive' effects of
> a society which permits free choice in welfare, one is back with
> 'integration' once more.... If we try to eliminate differences,
> the nations within which they exist would lose much of their
> energy and creative power. The suggestion that the people
> of these countries would be better by forcing them all to
> go to the same schools and the same doctors in organisations
> administered by bureaucrats under the sort of control that
> democratic governments permit is incredible in itself and
> dangerous because of the disappointment its realisation would
> give rise to.

Criticism of the free market has mainly concentrated on the injustice of the principle in operation. But what were originally simply social justice arguments in favour of state provision of an integrated system have now shifted to include (indeed, in many cases have been taken over by) efficiency arguments. Not only is public provision of an integrated system more just, it is also (and probably even more important) more efficient. In emphasising efficiency and by stressing the need to plan the educational system, the influence of economic principles is still dominant.

From social justice to efficiency criteria

An efficient organisation is usually seen to be one where the means and techniques used are the ones most appropriate for achieving the ends of that organisation. Efficiency involves a clarification of aims and goals and an assessment of the relative advantages and disadvantages of alternative means. If the ends of an organisation are made explicit and the organisation (together with other organisations with which it interacts) is subject to some form of central control, then the development of that organisation can be consciously planned.

Those in education who are concerned to apply efficiency criteria in order to assess various methods of organisation and administration of education, can be divided into two main groups. The two groups are distinguished primarily by their attitude towards planning the educational system. The first group includes the efficiency 'hard-liners'. These are educationalists who concern themselves with the role of education in economic growth, with how and to what extent the education system should be planned, and with the application of business efficiency criteria to the education system. The efficiency 'soft-liners' are those who are more concerned to stress the difference between education and other institutions and organisations but, because of the current demand for economic justification, find they have to argue the efficiency of such goals as equality or social justice. (Titmuss, 1971, argues that in the giving of blood, altruism is a more efficient means of organisation!)

The efficiency hard-liners are interested in planning the development of the education system. They admit the difficulty of such a project because the aims of the education system are not clear, because education is not and cannot be bought and sold in a market and because it is not clear what criteria can be applied to measure the efficiency of an education system. The 1967 Year Book of Education critically examines three main kinds of indicators which educational planners are increasingly using to determine how much education should be provided and what is the correct balance between different kinds of education (see Lauwerys, 1969).

The first is the social demand approach of which the Robbins Report on Higher Education is a good example. In this case, attempts are made to forecast the future demand for places, and allowance is made for demographic and social trends. It is assumed that to provide more education will automatically benefit the economy so that any additional cost will not be too heavy. Consumer choice is given a wide scope. 'This approach commends itself to those who favour a permissive social climate, who are attached to traditional cultural values and who work in societies where public opinion has great influence' (Blaug and Lauwerys in Lauwerys, 1969, p. 79).

The second is the manpower requirements approach. In this case the goal is that total production should grow as fast as possible even if personal choice has to be limited. The main difficulty lies in attempting to estimate ten years in advance, how much of any kind of skill the country will need. If the goal is narrowly defined and pursued, it could well defeat its object.

The third is often regarded as a refinement of the second and is known as the cost-benefit approach (Blaug, 1970). The idea is to work out the costs of various types of education and to compare this with the returns both to the individual and to the society. Educational expenditure is seen as an investment and a rate of return is calculated using standard investment appraisal techniques. The high expenditure on some forms of education is put against the higher productivity and earnings of educated people. For example, the costs of university education include the direct costs (teachers, buildings, grants, etc.) met by the state, and the indirect costs such as the income that students forego while they are studying. However, people educated at university make a greater contribution to the national output than those people with only a school education. This extra output is measured by the higher lifetime earnings of graduates and these earnings differentials are the returns to education. Within the education sector, social rates of return should be used to determine the allocation of resources. Thus, if educating scientists yields a higher rate of return than educating artists, more resources should be devoted to the former.

The main criticism of such an approach is that it is not at all clear that policy decisions in education, based on the rates of return, will result in a desirable pattern of educational expenditure. Even if we ignore the fact that the rates of return are only approximately correct, the most important point is, are they meaningful? It is doubtful that differential earnings reflect scarcity and even more doubtful that the observed differentials of the educated are in fact due to education.

Much interest is at present being shown in an American financial technique known as programme budgeting. The Department of Education and Science published a planning paper on the subject in April 1970, and a number of local authorities have shown an interest in applying it to their total budget or to individual committees. One of the main ideas behind programme budgeting is that it is supposed to enable its users to establish policy objectives by making possible the analysis of inputs and outputs. Recurrent and capital costs are not treated as separate entities but as part of a policy. One project of the Higher Education Research Unit of the London School of Economics has been concerned with policy objectives in educational planning (Armitage, Smith and Alper, 1970). The authors have attempted to construct a model of the education system to take account of the range of policy options which might become available at different stages of the education process (and also to take account of the uncertainty of some of the data). They show the consequences of allowing for such variation and set out in detail what the administrative and planning consequences would be if such changes came about.

It is questionable, however, whether programme budgeting can ever be used in the education system to any great extent. There are practical objections in that the statistical information necessary is not available; the statistics at present are geared to Department requirements and these may not be appropriate. A further objection is that there is no point in making long-term plans on a programme budgeting basis if the whole thing would have to be completely changed by a change of government or a change in governmental policy. But probably even more important, certainly in the present climate of educational debate, is the fact that the whole exercise is pointless unless educational standards and values are considered too. Certainly no programme budget or any forward planning measures could take account of the need to preserve an appropriate environment for the inbuilt development of the knowledge-ideal.

The majority of progressive educationalists do not agree that this hard-line application of business efficiency criteria is appropriate to the educational system. Most progressives are concerned to stress that the goals of education are so diverse and diffuse that any particular form of organisation cannot be judged 'efficient' and therefore appropriate in the way that this is done by means of cost benefit analysis for industrial organisations. However, the economy is the most important single institution in a capitalist industrialised society. The influence of economic models is widespread and education, like any other institution, must define its goals and set about achieving them in ways that are appropriate because they are efficient. Progressives in education have come to believe that efficiency is the most important principle in a technologically based society. This has resulted in a curious shift whereby a number of organisational techniques in education, designed and promoted originally because they were more just and therefore desirable, are now promoted because they are more efficient and therefore more desirable.

The notion of the 'wastage of ability' is a case in point. The question of whether ability has been 'wasted' is a touchy one since both the bright girl, who leaves grammar school at sixteen, marries early and raises a happy family, and the intelligent boy, who leaves school early but does well in establishing his own small business, would be included in the 'wastage' category. Early leaving is usually taken as a ready index of waste of ability. The question of early leaving was examined in a report of that name in 1954. The report concluded that the most potent factor correlated with early leaving was the child's home background. Deterioration from the best selection group at entry to grammar school was most common among unskilled and semi-skilled workers' children, while improvement from the bottom group at entry to high academic achievement was most common among professional and managerial workers' children. The 'wastage' that occurred was condemned because of the injustice involved. But by the time the Crowther Report was published in 1959, the reason for condemning the wastage from early leaving had already shifted. In the National Service Survey which was undertaken for the Crowther Report, in ability group one, containing the most intelligent 10 per cent of the population, 42 per cent of them had left school at sixteen or before. Including group two, which contained the next 20 per cent of intelligence, two-thirds had left at fifteen and up to 87 per cent had left a year later. A social analysis of the group showed that the greatest loss was among sons of manual workers. This wastage was condemned because of the inefficiency that results when recruitment to occupations in the professional and managerial class is not of the most talented children. The most recent Government Social Survey Reports on early school leavers (1968) and on the sixth form (1970 and 1971) all stress the inefficiency of wastage of talent in the social and occupational structure.

This group of educationalists accepts that education and the advancement of knowledge must be planned and controlled according to both individual and social needs. However, this acceptance of the need to plan is not a positive assertion of the appropriateness of business efficiency techniques to the education system, and there is a difference in this respect from the hard-line efficiency group.

Condemnation of market principles and economic models sometimes results in a strange unity among critics; strange because condemnation of the market has brought together individuals who could usually expect to be diametrically opposed to each other. Thus, for example, there are striking similarities between the two authors, Bryan Wilson in his book *The Youth Culture and* *the Universities* (1970) and Theodore Roszak in his *The Making* *of a Counter Culture* (1970). The main theme of Wilson's book is that industrial development and the pervasion of market principles into all areas of life have resulted in the growth of a youth culture which is culturally and morally impoverished. This culture has eventually pervaded the universities, the last vestige of the cultural tradition. The theme which emerges from Roszak's work (concerning the cultural context of the USA) is that for a section of young people today, the whole rationalist, market tradition has been discredited as a result of its bureaucratic and technocratic consequences. The main difference between the two authors lies in the attitude they take towards the youth culture alternative. Wilson condemns it and looks backward; Roszak welcomes the change and sees hope for the future in it. But both writers condemn the present-day obsession with the market principle; both are critical of the results of advanced capitalist production; and both condemn the present materialistic obsessions and praise instead the intimacy of personal relationships and community that are threatened by such processes. Two polar opposite viewpoints can occasionally achieve harmony against a third factor that threatens them both.

In summary, it seems, therefore, that the increasing importance of economic criteria has cut across all the main streams of educational thought. Within the education system the efficiency ethic has had considerable influence on official reports in education since the middle 1950s. It has also been the main justification for the support of policies of expansion, delayed selection and the change to comprehensive schools. Thus, in an economically assessed education system, wastage is the main educational problem. In a technological society, the maximising of ability at all levels is an economic necessity. The social justice requirement, that no barriers should prevent the individual from maximising his educational potential, is also more efficient. One group of educationalists asserts the need for a free market environment, of competitive supply and consumer choice within the educational system. On the other hand, educational progressives, having accepted the need to plan education and the development of knowledge in accordance with individual and social requirements, are divided amongst themselves. One group, having made planning their goal, has taken up the techniques and procedures of business efficiency experts in order to determine appropriate educational development. A second group has recognised the importance of planning and controlling the development of the education system and the advance of knowledge, but is concerned to stress the important differences, particularly relating to aims and goals, between education and other organisations. Having made such a stand, this group nevertheless has capitulated to justifying these goals in terms of the efficiency criteria of economic models.

This is also the case with research and knowledge production. The educational system has no monopoly over the development of knowledge and research; consider the research that is controlled and sponsored by industrial organisations. The pluralism of know-ledge-producing agencies promotes the operation of market forces on the limited supply of resources available, and the most obvious utility criterion is that of economic benefit. Centralisation of control and government interference in education and in economics generate sensitivity towards the economic return of knowledge. This feature of contemporary industrial societies has been ideolo-gised in 'technology' and the euphemism 'industrial needs'. Educa-tional institutions are induced to structure their goals in terms of the use to which knowledge can be put in the solution of material problems. Economic rationalisation produces rationalised know-ledge to the extent that means–ends connections between problems and their solution are sharpened.

Education has always had an economic basis, whether this was conceived in terms of consumer choice or government budgeting. As soon as we contemplate changes in the educational system we are faced with competing wants. It is a question of establishing priorities. This inevitably leads to considerations of social economy, desirable direction of development and the question of costing. There is the priority of education itself in relation to defence, public health, old age pensions and family allowances. Within education, proposals for expansion or change must have con-sidered and counted the cost of such proposals and the order of priorities. It is significant that, particularly since the Second World War, the central education authority has seen the necessity of appointing economists and social administrators to the member-ship of committees and advisory councils investigating educational problems. However, education is not only an instrument of the economy. As Morrish (1972) points out:

In the educational process something is provided and
consumed at the personality level which is not always
(indeed rarely) measurable even in educational terms, to
say nothing of economic terms. It may well be possible to say,
for example, that £3000 has been spent on John Smith's
education; in personality terms one might equally be able
to say that this was money well spent, but in economic terms
there will certainly be somebody always prepared, and perhaps

able to prove, that it was all 'a dead loss'. The real difficulty is to elicit a satisfactory set of economic criteria by which to measure educational production and consumption.

Fritz Machlup (1970, p. 5) has suggested that any educational effort is a waste if it does not contribute either to pleasure or to productivity. But here we are dealing with incommensurables. Pleasure is not something which can be measured anyway. But, since productivity in economic terms cannot be known until a man has almost finished his course, it is virtually impossible to predict this beforehand. Productivity must relate to the sort of society in which the individual is going to live rather than the one in which he is living at the present moment. We may be doing all the wrong things for a computerised and cybernetic civilisation. But, irrespective of the difficulties of predicting future economic requirements, future gains in economic productivity are not the sole or even the most important criterion for assessing educational effort.

Pressures for economic rationalisation and efficiency are nourished by a predominantly business and industrial civilisation with its concern for profits, economic self-sufficiency and a materialist standard of living. It was economic pressure (the idea that education meant money) more than anything else that stirred governmental interest and increased governmental interference in education in recent years. Since the Second World War, this economic attitude has become dominant. It has the advantage over, and diverts attention away from, problems of social justice since it introduces a note of hard realism into a field otherwise characterised by vague theorising.

7

Class, status and power:
the management of knowledge

As long as intellectual life brings no tangible social or economic rewards, only those determined to pursue knowledge-ideals will turn to such a life. To the extent, however, that education and scholarship carry wealth, privilege and prestige, they will be desired by the mass of people. This does not mean that intellectual accomplishment will not be promoted, but that most people will desire the external trappings, the wealth, privilege and prestige, in addition to, or even instead of, the achievement of intellectual ideals themselves.

It is important to establish the extent to which income, status and power depend on performance in skills taught at school and on the achievement of educational certificates, degrees and diplomas. Wealth, status and power are directly related to the occupational structure: there is an increase in the wealth, status and power of positions as we move up the occupational hierarchy. Thus it is necessary to examine the extent to which occupational position is dependent on educational achievement.

In a meritocracy, economic, social and political rewards are distributed according to performance in intellectual accomplishments. Those who do best in the education system are allotted the most powerful, prestigious and best-paid positions in the occupational structure. Under conditions of perfect mobility, these positions would be reallocated in each successive generation. Everyone would have an equal chance of achieving a high position; the unequal distribution of talent would determine the ultimate allocation of positions. Under conditions of less than perfect mobility, individuals try to hold on to privileged positions; advantages are passed on to succeeding generations; high ranking positions become the preserve of certain social groups; social classes are formed and perpetuated.

Where educational achievements are used as selection criteria for elite occupational positions, the possibility exists of a merito-cratic system with high rates of social mobility. However, one of the effects of the operation of the educational system has been to perpetuate social and economic inequalities. The reasons for this arise partly out of the complex interrelationship between educa-tional achievements and social class background and partly because other than educational criteria are used in selection for elite occupational positions. Because of these reasons, education has been a major element in maintaining the existing social hierarchy.

Formal education, like tradition, generally tends to be dependent upon particular forms of social organisation. The changes in edu-cational outlook parallel the changes which a nation undergoes in the course of its history. The unifying factor in education reflects the dominance in each case of a given social body (for example, church, class or nation). Education can be described as the manner by which these social bodies perpetuate themselves from generation to generation. In so far as education is held responsible for the socialisation of children into the values, goals and accepted prac-tices of the society, the education system is a deliberate attempt to maintain and perpetuate the normative and action patterns of the society.

Educationalists disagree in their emphasis on the conserving and socialising functions of the educational system. Idealists see education as preserving and passing on all that is valuable in the culture, tradition and experience of past generations. Progressives, in contrast, see education as promoting desirable social changes. Education could play a positive part in reducing the inequalities and injustices of a class-bound society and encourage cooperation and unity of cultures and ideals. Such a dilemma inevitably in-cludes the larger question of the relationship between education and society. It involves the management of knowledge in order to promote a particular blueprint for the good society.

This chapter includes a consideration of two basic themes: firstly, the extent to which education and occupation (and hence education and class, status and power) are related; secondly, an explanation of how knowledge and the education system can be managed and organized to promote some conception of a desirable future society.

Education and occupation

Education is seen increasingly by parents as a means to get their children better jobs. This trend, together with the increasing demands of our society for highly trained specialists and for middle grade technicians, supervisory and clerical workers, has resulted in pressures for an educational response to meet the needs of the rapidly changing occupational structure. In industrial societies, schools perform the task of selecting and supplying new recruits to the labour force. They select and promote talent and ability, as and when required. In Britain, as in other modern economies, the education system is geared to the requirements of the labour market. Teachers are also recruiting officers and 'arbiters of life chances' (Maizels, 1970), and one of their main tasks is to grade and to classify the school population for different positions in the socio-economic hierarchy. Thus, the education system includes as one of its functions the sorting and selecting of individuals, according to its own educational criteria, between positions in the occupational hierarchy.

Education is playing an even greater part in the process of occupational and social mobility than it has done in the past. Olive Banks (1955) has claimed that: 'Opportunity to rise in the social and economic scale depends less and less upon the accumulation of small capital, more and more on the possession of degrees and diplomas.' Typologies of educational systems have been based on the selection function. (See, for example, Turner, 1960 and Hopper, 1968.) This situation is at least partly a result of structural changes in society, which have probably caused the drive for increased provision of education and have also tended to increase the demand on the part of employers for educational qualifications. Most people think of education as the means by which occupational positions are achieved. Education and occupation are inextricably interwoven concepts in the minds of the general public and upward social mobility is now acceptable and widely pursued. This does not mean there is no dispute concerning social mobility. The actual amount of social mobility and the importance of education as a mobility 'ladder' are both disputed. But perhaps what is important is that people *think* it is the main ladder. Thus, from the point of view of the individual, the education system is an opportunity structure.

Obviously, the relationship between the education system and the occupation structure is not a simple one. (For a discussion about this, see Floud and Halsey in Halsey, Floud and Anderson, 1961.) The growth of industrialism affects the demands the economy makes on the education system: technological change brings about the development of new occupations and the modification, decline or obsolescence of old ones. But education does not merely adapt to the changing needs of the economy. Changes in educational provision can influence the distribution of income between occupations. But even to the extent that the technical needs of the economy do mould the education system, the actual pattern of influence is mediated through educational theories, their interpretation by teachers and by the clash of various interest groups. In addition, the relationship may be distorted in peculiar ways as a result of special conditions such as large-scale unemployment or full employment, at particular times.

In general, however, as all educationalists will admit, in an industrialised economy the education system becomes an agency of occupational selection and mobility. Put differently, the greater the degree of industrialisation, the more young people are limited in their choice of employment by their educational attainments and the more difficult it is for adults to move outside the range of occupations for which their formal educational attainments equip them. Floud and Halsey (1961) have presented statistics relating to the association between type of secondary schooling, length of school life, further education and vocational choice. The majority of modern, technical and comprehensive school pupils leave school at fifteen. Of these, some three-fifths of boys under sixteen enter unspecified, unskilled and semi-skilled employment; about one-third enter apprenticeships for skilled crafts and about one in twenty go in for clerical employment. For those leaving school at sixteen or above, the superiority of their occupational distribution is marked. The proportion of boys at this age who enter apprenticeships is higher than among the under-sixteens while the proportion going into clerical work is much higher. A much higher proportion also enter employment or full-time further education leading to recognised professional qualifications. Of those who enter employment at seventeen, or later, of whom most have attended grammar schools, the proportion going into professional occupations, either directly or following further education, is considerably higher than among fifteen or sixteen year old school leavers (Carter, 1962). The main source of recruitment to the high status occupations in the professional and managerial class is the numbers of pupils in full-time further or higher education. In 1968, of the total age group of boys and girls aged eighteen plus, there were some 400,000 or 14 per cent of the age group in full-time education of all kinds. There were more than twice as many boys as girls in this group. Something like 220,000 or 8 per cent of the age group were in universities.

A complex relationship exists between the formal selection procedure within the education system and the fostering of different levels of vocational aspiration among children attending different types of school. A number of researchers (Himmelweit, 1952) have compared the 'dream' and 'anticipated' vocational aspirations of school children and occupational choices were found to be 'realistic'. Joan Maizels (1970) has been concerned with how the education system deals with the problem of recruitment for the unskilled labour force and the less pleasant work of society:

> It has been suggested that children who have to modify their choices and who are destined for the low status jobs, are more likely to accept their role if they have learned to regard themselves as relatively incompetent to perform jobs of higher skill and responsibility; if the prospect of even routine jobs seems more attractive than being at school; and if they believe that they are personally responsible for their decisions and that their employment is personally chosen.

A number of researchers have challenged the assumption that education is such an important element in social and occupational mobility. Ioan Davies (1970) has declared that it is inconceivable that educational selection be studied independently of the total selection process within any society:

> It might be found, for example, that although the educational system is highly centralised and stratified, the selection of people depends also on internal recruitment and in-service training. Conversely, although education may be deliberately selective and related to man-power requirements, many of the trainees may find themselves without jobs or with jobs at variance with their qualifications because of mobility features within industry and commerce.

Gosta Carlsson (1958) has claimed that good schooling is a great asset to those who have it but, taking the overall picture, it is by no means the major influence in any upwardly mobile group. Carlsson examined mobility data in a rather different way from that of other researchers. In most cases, a cross-section of the population is examined and education is correlated with occupational position. Carlsson's method was to look at an upwardly mobile group as a cohort and describe it in educational terms. Similarly, C. Arnold Anderson in a paper entitled 'A Sceptical Note on Education and Mobility' (in Halsey, Floud and Anderson, 1961), examines the contention that social mobility is closely dependent on formal education. Using data from Glass's study in Britain (1954), Centers' work in the USA (1949), and Carlsson in Sweden (1958), Anderson examined the statistics of the educational achievements of an upwardly mobile group. As a result, he points out that some sons with low educational achievements lose status far less often and those with intermediate or higher levels of educational achievement rise far less often than would be the case if education were the sole determinant. The least educated sons made many more up and fewer down moves than would be expected on the basis of their schooling alone. But they did make fewer up and more down moves than chance would bring about. Similarly, the best educated sons made fewer up and more down moves than education would bring about but their upward moves are more frequent and their downward moves less frequent than chance would produce. He concluded that education was but one of many factors influencing mobility but it was far from being a dominant factor.

It is probable that there is no real contradiction here. Carlsson and Anderson have pointed out that education has not been the only or even the most important factor influencing mobility in society. But because of the method used, their results are partly attributable to the very low proportion of individuals obtaining anything but elementary education. The corollary of this is that as the proportion of individuals with higher education increases in society, so the importance of education in the upwardly mobile cohort will increase.

So, education selects the recruits for different social positions. This is one of the principles of meritocracy. It is a basic, defining characteristic of meritocracy that access to the most important, powerful, prestigious and best paid occupations and positions should be reserved for the most intelligent and best educated. Thus, it is accepted that the education system becomes a sieve of ability, distributing occupational and social rewards according to its own definition of intellectual merit. But there are sharp differences in the conclusions that are drawn from the fact of this relationship. Many idealists in education, having argued the case for selection as an educational 'good', go on to acknowledge the importance of the function of education as an occupational and social selector. Education is perhaps the best institution to do this, idealists argue, if intelligence and achievement are to be the selection criteria, since the education system has the tools to hand. This additional function can do no harm to the education process provided the goals of education itself, such as the maintenance of the knowledge-ideal and standards of academic excellence, continue to be valued first and foremost. Idealists admit that there are dangers, however, in that these educational goals may be displaced by vocational aims if the education system becomes solely an instrument of the economy.

Many progressives are less certain of the relevance and competence of educational selection criteria and of the appropriateness of these criteria as determinants of occupational position. They are well aware that selection in education can determine economic and social position as well as the life styles and life chances of future generations. Progressives do not acknowledge that selection is important for the education process itself and would delay occupational and social selection as long as possible because of the consequences for the social and occupational positions of individuals.

In so far as occupation is linked to the status and power orders of society, and education is related to occupation, then education will also be linked to the status and power orders. Education continues to attract a high 'symbolic value', in addition to its 'functional value'. The 'symbolic' and 'functional' values of education are distinguished by R. Havighurst (in Halsey, Floud and Anderson, 1961). Education has a functional value when it is used directly to accomplish a purpose; thus, a doctor takes a medical course and becomes a doctor. Education has a symbolic value when it is used as a symbol of status, as when an uneducated but successful father sends his son to a public school, before the son enters the family business. In other words, the educated man is allotted a position high in the status hierarchy irrespective of his wealth and power. Learning and education continue to command high respect and even deference. The symbolic value of education continues to be great. Nowhere is this better shown than by the continuing distinction, emphasised by idealists, between liberal and vocational subjects. The conception of a gentlemanly, non-utilitarian, largely ornamental education is still pervasive and carries with it respect and high prestige. The traditions of scholarship mean a great deal to the educated public and are regarded with deference by the rest. No doubt vested interests are important; established statesmen, judges, administrators, headmasters and other members of the Establishment were themselves educated in the traditions of scholarship and they attribute their success in life partly to this fact. The idea that education is important in developing a disciplined character first became prevalent in the public schools during the nineteenth century and it continues today in the high status grammar and private sector schools. This has general application in that it resulted in the theory that, in adult life, the liberally educated amateur is to be preferred to the vocationally trained specialist. Thus, whatever its intrinsic merits, the idea of a liberal education continues to include an esoteric mystery which helps to make it awe-inspiring in the eyes of the general public. There is no doubt that the association of a liberal education with famous educational institutions and with superior social occupations gives it a unique prestige in the community.

The more egalitarian society becomes, the less sympathy there is for such traditional concepts of status. Idealists continue to stress the symbolic value of education and in doing this they are open to the criticism of trying to maintain old and outworn power hierarchies. The unequal distribution of power, defined as the ability to control the behaviour of others, especially the control of groups over the life chances of others, is linked with occupational and status factors. If education functions as a selector for the occupation and status structures, it also functions as a selector for the power structure or the 'power elite' and this increases the importance and the symbolic value of the educational process. It is possible to see education as an important instrument for the manipulation of individuals, both in its role as socialising agent and in the functions it fulfils for the society in selecting recruits for the top positions. Knowledge can be managed in order to promote some ideal conception of a desirable future society.

The management of knowledge

All societies have a dominant condition or problem, or a central political theme that gives shape to the economy and the state and therefore to the educational system. In South Africa the dominant problem is race relations. Everything about South African society is affected by the race problem. The government makes this its major concern. The economy is built on a system of race-related division of labour. The state controls the educational system to ensure that it serves the national policy of race relations.

The National Socialist regime in Hitler's Germany provided an example of a dominant political theme giving shape and direction to the educational system. (Hans, 1949, considers the influence of the secular traditions of Humanism, Socialism and Nationalism on educational systems.) Nothing but the total subordination of the individual to the national ideal as defined by the Nazi doctrine could lead any German to the pinnacles of power and material well-being. Those German youths who had the necessary racial qualifications and were ready to follow the prescribed path were selected as future leaders and were educated apart from the masses. Thus the Nazi educational system was divided into two school systems: one for the masses, training them to blind obedience, and the other for the leaders, training them to rule and command as faithful paladins of the Führer. Both systems of education were based on political indoctrination. All school subjects were 'cooked' and presented to the rising generation in a perverted form. Measures were taken to prevent any other information reaching the children. History and literature suffered most; everything was presented from the 'racial' point of view.

In Russia, after the revolution of 1917, there was a new set of ideals for the society, a new set of goals with a new kind of leadership. The educational system, too, had to be made over to fit the new society. Since Russia's educational system is a development of the state and the economy working together, education is planned to keep in step with and to be an instrument for economic development. The most striking illustration of this is the areas of specialisation of university students. In Russia 70 per cent of university students study engineering or science subjects, those which have the most obvious instrumental value for economic development. Since Russian society is formed around the principle of cooperation in a variety of collective organisations, the schools are designed to serve the purpose of making the child an effective member of the collective team. In a collective economy there must be competition among factories and among workers, in order to maintain high achievement motivation. At the same time, there must be a high degree of conformity to collective decisions and to cooperative forms of organisation.

In all societies with a formalised, state organised educational system, education is designed to promote specific political and social goals. In socialist countries, like Russia, with its socialist economy and ideology, education clearly means training in dialectical materialism and socialism. In capitalist countries like the USA, where economic and political freedom are emphasised, education is equivalent to training in American traditions which are definitely anti-socialist. In Britain, also, education includes training in British traditions but strictly speaking this is neither socialist nor capitalist. Each teacher is free to develop his own arguments. However, an important part of the British academic tradition emphasised by idealists is to see the educational system stimulating, promoting and maintaining an intellectual elite as the guardians of a just and enlightened society in which knowledge and culture remain ultimate goals. Progressives in education envisage a rather different purpose for the education system. They see education playing an important part in promoting desirable social changes. Thus, a just education system and the adoption of egalitarian goals will mean the transference of such goals and values to the wider society.

All educational theories are political theories. All educational arguments and ideas contain value-assumptions and include visions of utopias. Usually, educational and social arguments are intertwined. What begins as an educational issue (selection, for example) is debated in social terms (selection is unjust because middle class children are selected and working class children are not). What is justified as an educational argument is really a social argument: social equality is the real point at issue.

We need to examine this notion of education as knowledge-management. Education is a powerful instrument of social control that can be used to promote almost any social goal. This also involves the analysis of the interrelationship between educational organisations and the economy, the power structure and the communications systems. It is necessary to examine how education is involved in both the creation and transmission of values and the way that the development and institutionalisation of knowledge and intellectual styles contributes to the social order, culture and tradition of any social structure. (Davies, 1970, talks about the development of national intellectual styles.)

Until recently, sociologists had hardly considered education as an instrument of social control. Michael F.D. Young (1971) has argued that this is because the *content* of education has not been examined, either in terms of how the educational system might influence publicly available meanings or how contemporary definitions of culture have consequences for the organisation of knowledge in the school system. Sociologists have accepted an absolutist conception of a set of distinct forms of knowledge which correspond closely to the traditional areas of the academic curriculum. For instance, by using a model of explanation of working class school failure which justifies reformist social policies, they are unable to examine the socially constructed character of the education at which the working class children fail. This is to justify rather than examine the content of education. Young believes that what is needed is a framework for analysing how knowledge is stratified and how this is the socio-historical construct of a particular time and society.

Pierre Bourdieu (in Young, 1971, p. 175) considers that the social organisation of knowledge is best described not in terms of the 'structural' properties of events-in-the-world which the knowledge is intended to formulate, but rather as a product of the informal understandings negotiated among members of an organised intellectual collectivity:

> It may be the upper classes who, by their social standing,
> sanction the rank of the works they consume in the hierarchy
> of legitimate works. Also, it may be specific institutions such as
> the education system and academies which by their authority
> and their teaching consecrate a certain kind of work and
> a certain type of cultivated man. Equally it may be
> literary or artistic groups, coteries, critical circles, 'salons',
> or 'cafes' which have a recognised role as cultural guides
> or 'taste-makers'.

He argues that a plurality of social forces almost always exists in all societies, sometimes in competition, sometimes coordinated, which by reason of their political or economic power or the institutional guarantees they dispose of, are in a position to impose their cultural norms and educational philosophies on a larger or smaller area of the intellectual field. These social forces claim legitimacy for the cultural products they manufacture, for the opinions they pronounce on cultural products manufactured by others, or for the educational philosophies and ideologies they transmit.

Raymond Williams (1961b) has distinguished four sets of educational philosophies or ideologies which rationalise different emphases in the selection of the content of curricula. He relates these to the social position of those who hold them. Also he suggests that curricula changes have reflected the relative power positions of the different groups over the last hundred years.

Ideology	Social position	Educational policies
1. Liberal/ Conservative	Aristocracy/ gentry	Non-vocational— the 'educated man', an emphasis on character
2. Bourgeois	Merchant and professional classes	Higher vocational and professional courses. Education as access to desired positions
3. Democratic	Radical reformers	Expansionist— 'education for all'
4. Populist/ proletarian	Working classes subordinate groups	Student relevance, choice, participation

A stratified model of knowledge and a clearly defined hierarchy of value and worth are so much taken for granted by most educators that it is difficult to conceive of the possibility of knowledge which is not stratified. Our assumptions about the stratification of knowledge are implicit in our ideas of what education 'is' and what teachers 'are'. The contemporary British educational system is dominated by academic curricula with a rigid stratification of knowledge and a hierarchy of worth and value.

In any society, by what criteria are different areas of, kinds of and approaches to knowledge given different social value? These criteria will have developed in a particular social and historical context but may also be related to social, political and economic factors in accounting for changes, and resistances to changes, in curricula. The structure of the intellectual field may be more or less complex and diversified according to the society or the functional weight of the various authorities claiming to have cultural legitimacy. However, it is possible to postulate some of the common characteristics of academic curricula and attempt to show how, over a particular historical period, they have become legitimated as of high status by those in positions of power. These characteristics will apply whenever an intellectual culture exists which is relatively independent of the political, economic and religious authorities. But these characteristics are not absolutes; they are socio-historical constructs. M. F. D. Young (1971, p. 37) suggests as dominant characteristics of high-status knowledge:

> Literacy, or an emphasis on written as opposed to oral present-
> ation; individualism (or avoidance of group work or cooperative-
> ness ...); abstractness of the knowledge and its structuring and
> compartmentalising independently of the knowledge of
> the learner; finally and linked with the former, the unrelatedness
> of academic curricula, which refers to the extent to which
> they are 'at odds' with daily life and common experience.

It is not that these particular skills and competences are associated with highly-valued occupations, because some occupations 'need' recruits with knowledge defined and assessed in this way. Rather, it is suggested by Young that any very different cultural choices, or the granting of equal status to sets of cultural choices that reflect variations in terms of the suggested characteristics, would involve a massive redistribution of the labels educational 'success' and 'failure', and thus also a parallel redistribution of rewards in terms of wealth, prestige and power. It would involve an examination of the relationship between education and social change and between social change and cultural change. Basil Bernstein (1970a) has elaborated the link between social change as conceived by Émile Durkheim (mechanical to organic solidarity) and cultural change (the move from collection to integrated type curricula).

The mechanical/organic distinction was made by Émile Durkheim in his *Division of Labour* to illustrate the different bases of social order and control in pre-industrial and industrial societies. Following Durkheim, Bernstein claims social control in society is no longer dependent, as it used to be, on the transmission of common values through ritual order or based on position and status. Appeal is no longer made to shared values and group loyalties (mechanical solidarity) and, as a result, the symbolic significance of punishment is weakened. Instead, control is now dependent on a recognition of individual differences (organic solidarity); control has become personalised. As a result, as far as the organisation of education is concerned, there needs to be a similar change. In the organisation of schools, there needs to be a move away from teaching groups as a fixed structural unit and towards a more flexible or variable unit of organisation. Under the old and outdated system of mechanical solidarity, the role of the pupil was fixed and ascribed such that aspirations were limited and individuals were related through common beliefs and shared sentiments which regulated details of social action. However, organic solidarity will involve more choice for all pupils. Aspirations will be raised because of changes in organisation. There will be greater individual autonomy and roles will be less clearly defined. They will evolve out of diverse contexts and relationships and will reveal differences not similarities. There will be a blurring of boundaries between school and non-school. Inside and outside school will be less clearly defined and non-school sub-cultures incorporated within the school.

In the old order, knowledge was 'sacred' and had to be confined to special well-chosen persons and divorced from practical concerns. The different forms of knowledge were bounded and well insulated. There needs to be a shift in the curriculum from the subject as a clear-cut definable unit to where the unit is not so much a subject as an idea. Bernstein has distinguished and compared 'collection' and 'integrated' curricula in an article 'On the Classification and Framing of Educational Knowledge' (Young, 1971). Bernstein claims that we need to change from concern with learning standard operations tied to specific contexts, to the exploring of principles. This implies a change in the teacher's role from teacher as solution-giver to teacher as problem-poser.

Bernstein points out that such changes will be seen as challenges to the old order of education. They will arouse abhorrence and disgust in educational guardians because they imply the dissolution of the old principle of social order. The new education would weaken authority systems and serve consensual (instead of elite) functions. In the past, education has been a process maintained by the ruling groups in order to legitimate their own positions, to enable them to absorb potentially able leaders from the lower orders and to manage to obtain the acceptance or acquiescence of less powerful groups. Bernstein gives the following reasons for the need to move towards institutionalising integrated codes: (i) growing differentiation of knowledge at higher levels of thought, together with integration of previously discrete areas; (ii) changes in the division of labour creating different concepts of skill; (iii) less rigid social structure of the integrated code making it potentially a code for egalitarian education; and (iv) advanced industrial societies, with a range of beliefs and ideologies, having a major problem of control. Inter-personal (rather than inter-positional) control of the integrated code may set up penetrating, intrusive forms of socialisation. The new education would meet the needs these changes bring about. The barriers between education and the outside world would be removed. The 'open school' would result in the open society. The academic culture would be absorbed into the common culture and education would become an instrument of social cohesion.

But how do we account for the criteria implicit in the different ways knowledge is formulated? We can hypothesise how relations between the economy and the educational system produce different degrees and kinds of stratification of knowledge. It is possible to trace a set of stages from a non-literate society where educational institutions were not differentiated from other institutions, to a feudal type society where formal education in separate schools was almost entirely restricted to a priestly caste. Then, through the church ownership of land, how such schools remained largely independent (at least regarding curricula) of the economic and political processes of the time. Gradually, however, schools and colleges became increasingly differentiated and dependent on the economy of the society and, at the same time, the dominant economic and political orders became the major determinants of the stratification of knowledge.

But it is important to be aware that to conceive of education as knowledge-management raises not only the question of what is possible in the way of socialisation but also what is *desirable*. It is necessary to consider how education is related to the social order of any social structure and the possibilities that exist for education to contribute to changes in that social structure. Durkheim (1956) urged that education 'consists of a methodical socialisation of the young generation'. Karl Mannheim (1936) had much the same notion in mind when he contended that 'by becoming society-conscious we no longer formulate the needs of Youth in the abstract, but always with reference to the needs and purposes of a given society'. Yet, in spite of the emphasis of both on the 'Society', there are considerable differences in the nature of the 'Society' for which they intended to prepare the young.

For Durkheim, society itself was the moral personality which lasted beyond generations and bound them together. Therefore, education was 'essentially a matter of authority', necessary in order to 'bring us to overcome our original nature'. Implicit in Durkheim's conception was a sense of stability in terms of which society provided both security and release from human powers. By and large he approved the values of his time and such a society was positively recommended.

Mannheim was more aware of change, of disintegration and of the need to emerge out of the crises into a new society. Education, in its social role, became indistinguishable from propaganda, a social 'technique'. This was also implicit in his conception of the sociology of knowledge and the intimate relationship between thought and action. The emphasis on change rather than on stability in society resulted in the conception of education as an instrument for bringing about a new social order rather than as a means for introducing children to the values of the present society. 'The rate of transformation can ... be accelerated, if deliberate changes in education are planned, corresponding to the parallel social tendencies in the same direction.'

In attempting to understand the disputes between the progressives and the idealists in education, it is necessary to examine their attitudes to the relationship between education and social change. If the school is required to perpetuate and transmit the signs and values of academics and scholars, and if conformity and deviance, success and failure are defined in these terms then, as many progressives argue, for large numbers of pupils, such a conception will be in conflict with other cultural values which surround them —modern communications media, for example. If the educational system is seen to be an institution specially contrived to conserve, transmit and inculcate a particular value and order system, then it will derive a number of its structural and functional characteristics from the fact that it has to fulfil these particular functions.

Education is involved in both the creation and transmission of values. The institutionalisation of a particular knowledge-ideal contributes to the social order, culture and tradition of the social structure. An educational system is ultimately defined by its historical and political contexts. It is from these contexts that the problems of organisation and structure, of curriculum and content, derive their meaning. An educational system is a generalised expression of the human, social and moral concerns of its time and place. Educational theories reflect the range of alternative possibilities regarding the education and society, social order and social control relationships. In other words, contrasting educational theories and alternative educational systems pose value dilemmas. Obviously ethical arguments about these values cannot be settled by educationalists since this would be circular. But it is to say that social and political values play a very pervasive role in education through the management of knowledge and the institutionalisation of intellectual styles. By defining success and failure, conformity and deviance, the educational

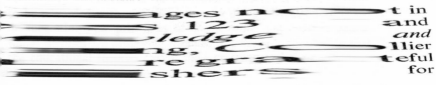

8

System and action models: the sociological dilemma

This book has so far been concerned to elaborate the major socio-political dilemmas that arise because of different and usually conflicting interpretations of basic educational concepts. It is one of the main contentions of this book that there is a certain patterning in these different interpretations such that, for example, a particular model of intelligence 'fits' with a particular conception of education, and this in turn is associated with a perceived desirable relationship between education and the total society. It is claimed, further, that such dilemmas are also related to dilemmas of structure and organisation in such a way as to highlight the interrelationship between educational ideas and structures, and between educational structures and politico-economic institutions.

It is proposed in this chapter that these basic dilemmas are mirrored in the discipline of the sociology of education itself. It is suggested that there are two distinct models used by sociologists looking at education and that the sociology of education, as it appears today, has developed out of the conflict between them. (The contrast between the two approaches and the implications for sociology in general have been discussed in two articles: Silverman, 1968 and 1971; Dawe, 1970.) The system and the action approaches posit antithetical views of human nature, of society and of the relationship between the social and the individual. The educational dilemmas which mirror major socio-political dilemmas are also reflected in a dilemma within the sociology of education itself concerning choice of model, concepts and perspective.

In fact, it is possible for sociologists to look at education from one of three perspectives. Firstly, there is the approach which stresses the interrelationship of the system of education with other institutions of society such as stratification, the family, the economy. In this case it is appropriate to talk about wider social demands or the 'needs' of other institutions and the 'functions' of the education system. Secondly, there is the approach which sees education as an enclosed system and therefore most usefully approached from the perspective of organisation theory. Thirdly, there is the approach which sees education in the light of a social action model, drawing on Weber's notion of social action through the use of an ideal-type of 'rational' action. Such a model enables an examination of the extent of conflict that may exist between different ends and the role of power in determining outcomes. For our purposes, the first two perspectives can be collapsed and the 'system' and 'action' approaches to education compared.

It is suggested that the social action model is more appropriate to the progressive conception of the education process. The progressives see education centred on the child and on the child's own conception of his needs and interests. This involves an attempt to understand the child's own perception of goals and ends, and enables an examination to be made of the extent of the conflict that may exist between different perceived ends. The idealist is more interested in the knowledge-ideal as the ultimate value of the education system. Therefore the idealist can talk of the requirements of the education system and can compare the functioning of different types of structure and institutions to achieve this end.

Education as a social system

A social theory of education is often assumed to be one concerned with hypothesising a 'fit' between a model of society and a model of an educational system. In such a case, the sociologist of education is concerned with developing macro-level models. The most obvious instances of such models are the social theories of education developed by Durkheim and Mannheim, and contemporary functional analyses of education.

It has been popular among sociologists to conceive of 'society' as something external to the individual and exercising constraint over him. (The alternative is to see society as a reflection of man's goals and interests and therefore shaped by him.) The former is the approach adopted whenever education (or any other institution) is referred to as a 'system'. This is the case whether or not they have been explicitly functionalist. Education is thought of as an institution which has a 'goal' and this 'goal' is related to the wider social system, the society. In addition, this 'goal' is something more than the sum total of the goals of its individ[ual] [mem]bers. Also, the education system has certain 'needs' w[hich must] be met if it is to continue to pursue its goal and the [...] 'survive' and continue to 'function' for the wider society [...] then centres around the mechanisms whereby needs ar[e ...]

The table and certain pa[...] quotation marks on pa[...] 124 are taken from *K[nowledge and] Control*, Michael F D Y[oung,] Macmillan (1971), and w[e are indebted] to the author and pu[blisher for] permission for their use.

functions performed.

Obviously, there are difficulties in this position and often these have resulted in a general condemnation of the systems approach to society. By talking about the 'needs' of an education system and about the functions it performs for society, firstly we are creating an artificial structure, a 'system', and drawing boundary lines around it; and secondly, we are attributing human motivations and characteristics ('needs', 'purposes' and 'functions') to this artificial structure. In other words, we are 'reifying' the system (Berger and Luckman, 1967, develop the notion of 'reification'.)

In addition, system theories have difficulties in dealing with problems of deviance and disorganisation. The most common method of dealing with such phenomena is to introduce the concepts of stress and strain to explain problems in organisation. Thus, when students revolt or education's functions are not performed, this must be because the system is not flexible enough (or tough enough). Conflict stems from bad communications, difficult personalities or too many conflicting demands from the wider social system. But conflict is neither endemic nor insoluble; effective organisation can reduce and even eliminate it (Rice, 1970). Consensus is the normal state in system theories.

Many of the difficulties posed by system theories stem from the need to relate the educational system to the wider social system. Functional theories suggest how the educational system works towards the fulfilment of societal goals, usually the stability and continuance of the society. Since Merton (1957), it is not necessary to see every aspect of the education system as positively functional for the society. Merton has distinguished 'latent' as well as 'manifest' functions, 'dysfunctions' as well as functions, and 'functional alternatives' instead of the universal functionality of all parts of the system. Coser (1965) has indicated how conflict can have latent functions or unintended functional consequences for a society or for any institution.

Talcott Parsons (1951) takes the integration of the individual into the system as his main concern. Integration of the educational system is achieved by providing motivation to individuals, teachers and pupils, to carry out their organisational roles. People play their organisational roles because they have internalised the norms which are basic to the roles, because they seek the approval of others and desire the goals that are the rewards of successful role-playing in the educational system.

The system model involves the reification of the educational system and attribution of needs, goals and functions to it. One of the main consequences of such reification is that the effectiveness of any particular school structure or organisation can only be measured by reference to the needs of the system or the needs of the society. In addition, conflict can only be considered in terms of system goals and the causes of conflict are attributed to poor organisational means such as lack of fit between role and personality. Talcott Parsons ('The School Class as a Social System', *Harvard Educational Review*, 1959, vol. 29) distinguishes two goals of the school: role socialisation and status socialisation. This gives rise to the following question: do teachers and pupils see the organisation as preparing its output with skills to do particular jobs or social skills to behave in ways appropriate to particular positions? But perhaps neither of these goals is immediately important to either teachers or pupils.

Application of an educational system model results in a good deal of confusion between the system's goals and the goals arising from the system's interrelationship with the wider society. The wider social system includes not only all other systems and institutions but also the history and traditions of the system itself. Etzioni (1961) has suggested that it is possible to distinguish between on the one hand goals which are derived from power and structural situations extrinsic to the system itself, and on the other those which are derived directly from the system's own norms, values and traditions. In some societies, educational goals might be directly derived from the wider social system. In others, they may derive much more from the educational system itself. One of the major factors in determining the goals of the educational system will be the power structure in the society and in the education system. However, studies based on system theories tend to acknowledge power aspects and communications mechanisms without having anything to say about the sources of the values and knowledge being transmitted. System theory results in a consideration only of the *consequences* of the use of power for the system, never does it result in a concern with the *causes* of the distribution of power. With any system analysis it is necessary to note the degree of compliance in relation to both political and economic policy goals and also to subcultural norms and values. The extent to which education is able to counter the policies of a political elite will depend partly on its own economic independence, partly on educational socialisation being strong enough to resist the norms of the wider system (where these are different) and partly on the existence of local centres of political power which are able to give backing to the pursuit of alternative policies. Within particular educational systems there may be considerable institutional variation (between primary schools and universities, for example) in terms of compliance with different goal emphases and the degree of reliance on particular sub-cultural values and norms. The tendency of system models, however, is to limit interest in the wider system to what are perceived to be the needs of the educational system itself.

Also, such a position leads to the Parsonian view that all systems have a tendency to 'boundary maintenance' within a 'moving equilibrium'. The educational system will respond to internal and external threatening influences by attempting to absorb them and restoring itself to a state of equilibrium. The educational system will attempt to preserve its character in spite of growth and adjustment. If value consensus is important in ensuring the integration of any system, whether the total social system or a subsystem, this implies that social change occurs primarily because of a new external factor to which the system adjusts. This tends to preclude any consideration of how pressure for change can arise within the educational system because of conflicts of interests and of power balances.

For many years, the sociology of education has been concerned to elaborate a system theory of education and of the relationship between education and society. The central concern of such studies was with the structure of the educational system and the relationship between education and other institutions of society (family, religion, stratification, etc.) and society itself (education as socialisation, education as social selector). The majority of general textbooks in the sociology of education adopted just such an approach, especially those intended for college of education students. (See, for example, Banks, 1968; Musgrave, 1965; Swift, 1969; or, more specialised, Eggleston, 1967; Hoyle, 1969.)

One particular branch of system theory, a theory of organisations, has also been applied to the sociology of education. Organisation theory is an attempt to develop a general theory applicable to all types of organisations, industrial or otherwise, to provide a systematic basis for the study of the common characteristics of all organisations. The aim, then, is to provide a general theory of organisations applicable to such diverse institutions as a school, a hospital and a factory. P. W. Musgrave (1968) has analysed the school as an organisation. He summarises his book in the following way:

> We have defined organisational activity as purposeful. For this reason the first task in this book will be to specify the goals of contemporary education.... We must look at the overall structure of the educational system. This forms a major part of the environment within which individual schools exist and also acts as a constraint upon the way any school interacts with other organisations or institutions....

The next step will be to examine the role of the head and the role of the teacher.... It seems a sociological rule that organisations come to lead something of a life of their own, independent of their stated purposes. In any analysis of the working of such a complex organisation as a school the nature of these important internal processes must be discerned. Only in this way is it possible to counteract forces that may divert the school from achieving its goals.

Using a similar organisational model, A. K. Rice (1970) has examined each of the different tasks inherent in the objectives of the university and has described a model organisation best suited for the performance of these tasks:

A central concept used in the analysis is that of the 'primary task'. This is defined as the task that any institution or sub-institution must perform if it is to survive. The concept is related to a theory of organisation that treats any institution or sub-institution as an open system, that is, a system that depends for its existence on a continuous exchange of materials with its environment. The first theme of this book is that universities are multiple task institutions; and that each task, though interdependent with other tasks, requires its own characteristic organisation which differs from the organisation required for other tasks and for the whole. The second theme is that concentration on the interdependence of the tasks has tended to obscure their independent values, with consequent confusion of tasks, boundaries of activity systems, roles and role relationships. In effect, because of expansion the 'community of scholars' has become differentiated into a number of sub-communities with diverse and often conflicting interests. The third theme is that present university organisation is based for the most part on closed-system characteristics, in which transactions with the environment are kept to a minimum.

Organisational theories of education highlight the problems inherent in the system approach generally. Here, as before, there is a reification of a functional educational system. Emphasis is placed on the goals of the educational system and efficient task fulfilment is judged in these terms. Conflict is seen to result from inadequate organisational structures and power is to be considered merely as a resource to be used in the attainment of the educational system's goals. Flexibility is necessary to ensure system survival

133

in the face of change and system 'needs' must continue to be met to ensure efficient fulfilment of system tasks.

For the more traditional educationalist, the pursuit of knowledge and the maintenance of standards of academic excellence and scholarship are the goals of the educational system. In addition, education socialises new members into the values and ideals of the society and in this way contributes to the stability and equilibrium of the total social system. Organisation theory or a more general system theory provides a model for such an analysis. Alternative educational structures and organisations can be judged and compared in terms of their efficient functioning towards these ends. Conflict is seen to result only from inadequate institutional structures. The 'needs' of the educational system in terms of adequate resources and selected recruitment will ensure efficient fulfilment of the system's functions, such as maintenance of academic ideals and effective socialisation of new entrants into the occupational and social system.

However, in recent years, the need for a model of education and of society based on change rather than stability, and characterised not by consensus but by only a limited integration between institutions, has resulted in the search for a new approach (Floud and Halsey, 1958):

> Equilibrium—even if interpreted dynamically, is a difficult notion to apply to industrialised societies. They are dominated by social change, and consensus and integration can be only very loosely conceived with regard to them.

The difficulty of ascribing 'ends' or 'needs' to the educational system has been acknowledged by some researchers and the attempt abandoned. Instead, they suggest the 'ends' and 'goals' as perceived by participants as the starting point for analysis. This approach is generally known as the 'social action' or the 'interactionist' model.

Education: a social action model

According to Max Weber (1947), the notion of 'action' plays a central part as one of the fundamental concepts of sociology. A defining characteristic of action, for Weber, is its 'meaningfulness'. The notion of 'meaning' played a large part in the debate about the methodology of the social sciences in Germany before Weber's time. The sense in which he used the term was primarily to refer any particular behaviour to the purpose or aim of a hypothetical actor. This is the rational type of action (i.e. when behaviour is understood simply as a means to an end) and although Weber does not confine himself to this type, he uses it as a starting point so that other types can be understood in terms of their deviation from the rational pattern. Weber classified actions into four main types: Zweckrational; Wertrational; traditional; and affectual. This diversity of motivation has been the concern of many sociologists since Weber (Cohen, 1968). However, the use of an ideal type of rational action enables a systematic analysis of behaviour to be made which is both sociological (thus overcoming psychological reductionism criticisms) and objective (thus overcoming criticisms that theories based on subjective concepts such as human motivations, involve abandoning principles of scientific proof).

Applying this to the sociology of education, there is a clear difference between action theory and the system approach. For an action theorist, the analysis of education always means analysis in terms of the motivation of a hypothetical actor. The organic approach is rejected together with any attempt to treat systems as wholes or to talk of the 'survival' or 'needs' of the educational system. It is the motivation of individuals, teachers and pupils, and not some vague category of the 'needs of the social structure' which is seen as the ultimate determinant of any behaviour occurring within the educational system. The notion of 'function', too, is irrelevant except in so far as the term function can be used to describe the role of any particular action in the total plan of action of an individual. For it is from the motivation of that individual that analysis of the educational system begins.

This is not to assimilate sociological and psychological explanations. A simple psychological explanation would describe human behaviour in terms of what effect an individual's own motivation had on his overt behaviour. The sociological explanation includes the notion of an interactionist system whereby the behaviour of one individual, a teacher, can be determined by the pattern of motivation of another individual, his headmaster. The great advantage of this is that it frees us from the consensus framework of system theory. It permits an analysis of the extent of conflict that may exist between different ends and the part that power plays in determining outcomes.

Further, behaviour is not explained just because it maintains the educational system. No longer is the system reified and assigned 'needs', 'functions' and 'goals'. The educational system is not an absolute, rather, it is relative to a particular balance of interests. Thus, behaviour in schools would not be explained in terms of the external controls and sanctions of the educational system. Rather, the controls and sanctions would themselves be explained (Rex, 1961):

135

in terms of the necessity of certain behaviour to the continued existence of an (educational) system based upon a particular pattern of motivation. The 'external' facts which Durkheim correctly saw as being the sociological determinants of human behaviour lay not in the controls and sanctions, but in the demands which A's plan of action laid upon B. The controls and sanctions were themselves indirectly determined by these demands.

The action approach enables an analysis to be made of motivations of teachers and pupils directed to non-system ends. It is possible to relate the consequences of any action to the ends pursued by different groups rather than to any reified educational system. Also it is possible to examine whether any particular action leads to the attainment of an individual's or a group's end or hinders its attainment; what are the consequences for the ends pursued by other groups and individuals and how is the balance of power affected over time.

The notion of 'interaction' as a sophistication of the simple action model enables a certain amount of reconciliation to be made between the action and system approaches. Its great value is that it enables the unintended consequences of individual teachers' and pupils' actions to be examined. Action by itself emphasises only individual or group intentions. Interaction also emphasises the fact that most intentions also create consequences which were not intended. 'As soon as one actor must take into account the actions of another, he is no longer master of his own destination' (Cohen, 1968). Interaction indicates how different features or parts of the educational system are interrelated while at the same time avoiding reification and teleology in explaining how educational structures and systems operate. For the interaction approach does not assume that all action is structured or part of the education system, although it does assume that all educational structures and systems are the products and the conditions of interaction.

However, theories and models of action and interaction do not enable much to be derived from them about the nature of educational structures and educational systems. Obviously, this is because the content of interaction is governed by the educational structure or system in which it takes place. This circularity of argument is a basic criticism of the action approach to the sociology of education. The social situations in education are the product of action, and action is governed by the situation and by the culturally accepted modes of perceiving and reacting to those situations. If social phenomena in education are explained in terms of the structure of educational situations, including the actor's subjective view of these, then it is assuming what is to be explained. The action approach can help to explain the nature of social situations in education and how they affect conduct. It will not explain the educational structure and culture as such (Cohen, 1968, p. 94):

> The conclusion that action theory, in itself, explains very little, is valid. Action theory, as such, is a method. It is a set of near-tautological assumptions which structure the mode of cognition of social enquiry, which is, on the whole, concerned with the conditions and the products of social interaction.

A number of examples of the social action method as it has been used in the sociology of education will clarify what is at issue here. It is primarily a question of the starting point for analysis: the individual's perceived goals and his motivation to achieve them, or the functioning of the educational system and the interrelationship of institutions.

The action approach is often presumed to be a recent trend, though rooted in the work of classical sociologists such as Weber. Certainly its popularity in the sociology of education is fairly recent but as long ago as 1932, W. Waller, in his *Sociology of Teaching*, described the school as existing in a state of perilous equilibrium based on the balance of power within it. Compliance was achieved as exchanges of power resources took place between those in and connected with any school. Pupils exchanged good behaviour for freedom from sarcasm and other punishments. Similarly, teachers were free to teach as they thought best as long as parents, the headmaster and the local authority were guaranteed a high pass rate in external examinations. Power was exerted by the head over his staff, by the staff on individual teachers, by teachers over pupils and by pupils over other pupils. Teachers and pupils who exerted power had resources which they used to gain or wield power and they could follow different styles in doing so. The compliance that follows the successful use of power has been categorised by A. Etzioni (1964) under three headings: (i) compliance through coercion—corporal punishment and detention for example; (ii) normative compliance which depends on socialising pupils into the school's norms and inducing them to take on the role of good pupil; (iii) utilitarian compliance which refers to the power of the school to provide useful services which may be withheld.

Conflicts of values, goals and perceived interests in the classroom are predictable and indeed institutionalised. The class know just how far they can go before they will be punished. The first few meetings of a class with a new teacher will soon establish these limits. The class know the type of punishment that is appropriate for the level of disorder they have reached. The teacher has learnt the limit at which he must take action, but that any attempt to punish too severely is a violation of an unwritten but binding rule between him and the class.

John Holt's descriptions in his book *How Children Fail* (1970) show the way in which acting docile, playing at looking attentive, even acting stupid, are used by pupils to avoid humiliation. The lower streams support each other in this performance. At school, children are called upon to play the good pupil role which is based on academic and moral criteria upheld by teachers and others. Sanctions are brought to bear on pupils, but children bring latent roles into school that may hinder their acceptance of the role of good pupil. Those who are judged to succeed are allocated to the positions that the teachers and headmaster see as having prestige. Teachers create such positions in their classrooms in accordance with their own goals, and they use their power to try to make their pupils play the good pupil role as they define it. 'Deviance' is almost inevitable but it can be reinforced if the teacher labels the deviant as such. A deviant sub-culture develops with its own system of rewards and expectations.

D. H. Hargreaves (1967) has shown the importance of the fact that children become members of a group of age mates, most often from the same stream. These groups have their own values, norms and status hierarchies which every member must take into account. Hargreaves distinguished three distinct sub-cultures among one year of a streamed secondary modern school. The A stream's culture he called 'academic'; high status was given to those who did well at school work; bad behaviour was condemned; briefcases, school uniforms and short hair were approved. The B stream culture was 'non-academic'; they aimed to have fun; they did not want to work too hard but saw the connection between doing well at school and getting a good job in the future. The C stream's culture was 'anti-academic'; for these pupils the school rewards (for example, going up a stream) were seen as punishments; normal punishments were seen as rewards since they gave a boy status in his own group. In low streams, academically oriented boys were regarded by their teachers as conformists whereas on the peer group level they were deviants; the 'difficult' boys, the deviants to the teachers, were the high status conformists on the peer group level. The tendency of teachers to evaluate pupils in terms of their own rather than peer group values had important repercussions. The teacher had little chance of eliciting the desired response from these high status but anti-academic boys because the rewards he offered were inferior to those offered by the peer group from which such boys derived their security and status.

Since the action approach has caught the imagination of many current researchers, a large number of research experiments have been conducted into the importance of individual and group goals and values and their effect on the education process. In the USA, in the 1950s, Morton Deutsch carried out an experiment to show the effects of a 'competitive situation' and a 'cooperative situation' on achievement, cohesion and other factors (Cartwright and Zander, 1953). A number of studies were done in the USA into the so-called 'climate of values' which existed among students in different schools, and the effect of the different value climates on achievement in school (Coleman in Halsey, Floud and Anderson, 1961). More recently, in this country, B. Sugarman (1970) has conducted a number of experiments into informal structures in the classroom. Much of this research has resulted in a search for 'pro-school' peer groups which would reward good conduct at the same time as they supported academic effort.

The notion of an interactionist system includes the idea that the behaviour of one individual can be determined by another individual's patterns of motivation. Thus the school is a place where all members are constantly evaluating each other's actions and modifying their own behaviour accordingly. In the act of social evaluation, forces come together from two directions: the evaluator brings his own standards and values and the evaluee exhibits his. (For example, a teacher likes to dress fashionably whereas his headmaster likes his teachers to be dressed smartly and soberly.) The resulting judgments of the evaluator will be based on a consideration of conflicting values inferred from clues picked up from the behaviour of evaluees and on their relative power positions. Goffman's stage analogy (1959) is relevant here. What goes on in schools is fundamentally a question of impression management. An individual can learn to manipulate a situation by deliberately fabricating the clues which his behaviour offers to people around him. (So, a teacher dresses in a sober manner because he desires promotion.)

In such cases, behaviour is not explained in terms of the external controls and sanctions of the educational system. Rather, the controls and sanctions would themselves be explained in terms of the particular pattern of an individual teacher's motivation. The controls and sanctions are themselves indirectly determined by the demands which A's plan of action lays upon B. The education structure is formed by regular patterns of behaviour relating to the motivations of individuals and to the relative power positions of the individuals involved.

It is at this point, however, that the action model gets into difficulties. It is impossible to distinguish the motives and rational actions of individual teachers and pupils (in the sense of relating appropriate means to desired ends) from the pressures of the group, institution or educational system. Decisions made by an individual and his perception of the social situation are all a function of the group processes in which the individual is enmeshed. An individual's action choices constitute patterns of behaviour which relate to a normative order of explicit and unwritten laws. Thus, all we can say is that the school provides an environment within which a cycle of mutual influence operates between each personality and its surrounding social processes.

It is apparent, however, that the social action model is more appropriate to the progressive conception of the education process. Progressives would see education centred on the child and on the child's own conception of his needs and interests. The social action model links the concepts of meaning and action, the notion of actors defining their own situations and attempting to control them in terms of their definitions. Also, it adds the dimension of interaction or relationship between actors: one actor will attempt to impose his definition upon other actors in that situation. But there is no postulate of consensus or, for that matter, of cooperation, conflict or constraint in education. The extent to which any situation involves any or all of these becomes an empirical question. However, it needs to be remembered that both the child's and the teacher's conceptions of their own situations are to a large extent determined by their membership and participation in certain groups, and ultimately in society where they will both be required to compete for access to high status positions and rewards. Even the actor's definition of his situation, his perceived needs and interests, are socially determined!

In this chapter, two alternative models used by sociologists concerned with education have been distinguished and described. Also, it has been suggested that each of these two models is related to a particular conception of the education process, 'progressive' or 'idealist'. In this way, the two approaches also mirror socio-political dilemmas in education. The progressive educationalist, stressing the need for child-centred education, will recommend learning by discovery, the integrated curriculum, the abolition of selection and streaming, and comprehensive secondary schooling, to enable the child's perception of his needs and interests to influence his learning. The idealist educationalist, with an eye to the maintenance of standards of excellence and of getting the best possible results, particularly from the bright child, will want to teach respect for his subject and to encourage the personal characteristics fitted to the pursuit of scholarship; he will favour selection and the promotion of an intellectual elite. Thus, on the methodological level, there is a clear relationship between an explanation or model and a set of value assumptions about education. Both of the approaches described are related to a particular conception of the education process. Each conception is in turn related to specific structural and organisational arrangements and to a perceived desirable relationship between education and society. It is of major importance to emphasise the relationship that inevitably exists between values and models, between ideals and explanations, between educational ideas and educational structures and institutions.

We are faced, therefore, with dilemmas of educational aims, social philosophies, organisational means and conceptual interpretations. All these are dilemmas of value. In a very significant sense, all contain utopias and it is from these utopias that they derive meaning and justification. There are no easy solutions to these fundamental dilemmas. Any choice will involve loss and disadvantage in the sense that it is not a 'right' choice confronting a 'wrong' one, but rather two highly regarded values between which a choice has to be made. The main purpose of this book has been to elaborate the dilemmas that exist and to show the connections between them. In the final chapter, a number of important questions will be raised arising out of these dilemmas: who agrees with and who opposes particular definitions and interpretations? Who has the power to make these definitions effective in terms of appropriate educational structures and organisations? How do these definitions affect the processes at work within the organisations that are established? It is not suggested that we have answers to these questions. It is proposed, however, that to ask the questions in a way which emphasises the relationships between educational ideas and ideals, between concepts and structures, between models and solutions, is to move towards a genuine sociology of education rather than to rest content with a sociology of educational institutions which is only a part of the story.

9

Educational ideas in policy and practice

The world of education presents the spectacle of a battlefield of warring parties, conflicting doctrines and alternative models. Not only does each conflicting faction have its own set of interests and purposes, but each has its own picture of the world in which the same objects are given quite different values and meanings. In such a situation, the possibilities of communication and agreement are minimal. In addition, a further obstacle to the achievement of any sort of consensus in education is the obstinacy of the various partisans who refuse even to consider or take seriously the theories of their opponents, simply because they belong to another intellectual or political camp. This state of affairs is made even more complex by the fact that the educational world is far from free of the struggle for personal distinctions and power.

Thus we have a situation where a number of real dilemmas and moral alternatives—difficult enough in themselves—have become overlaid by considerations of ideology, vested interests and power politics. What needs to be done, therefore, is to clarify the genuine moral dilemmas and then to relate these to the social forms they have taken in terms of the dialogues (and conflicts) that exist in the field of education. This is in one sense an exercise in the sociology of knowledge since it is to describe the value context in which educational decisions are made. However, we need to beware of the assumption that educational theories directly affect the thinking of policy makers since we wish to assess just how much influence educational theories actually have.

Anyone attempting to analyse the educational system and to assess what education is trying to do, is immediately faced with a whole series of dilemmas which defy solution. In all educational matters there are alternative (frequently conflicting) courses of action and systems of thought. Each appears to have its advantages and compensatory disadvantages. Any choice has genuine elements of tragedy in it, in the sense that it is not a 'right' choice confronting a 'wrong' one, but rather two highly regarded values between which a choice has to be made. There seems to be no way of retaining both since even compromise involves loss of perceived advantages.

We have already distinguished a number of educational dilemmas. Do we treat all children as if they were equal when in terms of educational achievement they clearly are not (the ideals of justice and equal opportunities), or do we group children of equal ability together so that each group can progress at its own rate (ideals of concern for individual differences and promotion of high standards). How do we regard 'intelligence'? Do we see it as a hierarchical arrangement of intellectual skills and abilities differentially valued (ideal of educational excellence), or as a misleading structure designed to differentiate individuals in terms of its own criterion of worth (ideal of social justice). How do we see the 'educated man'? Do we see him as an individualist, an independent moral agent, self-reliant and suspicious of accepting the judgment of others in intellectual, moral and political matters? Or do we see him as part of a disciplined community of scholars dedicated to furthering the knowledge-ideal? How do we regard the 'knowledge-ideal'? Do we see it as a social value in its own right, the ultimate goal of all educational processes, or as a 'reified' construct designed to make education a straitjacket and an outdated reproduction of itself? Should the school reflect what it considers to be society's dominant values, or should it educate its pupils to regard them sceptically or even to reject them? Society is hierarchical; should the school classify its pupils accordingly? Society is competitive; should the school exemplify the pursuit of success? Is the main responsibility of the school to initiate its pupils into a common culture or should it be orientated towards the occupational structure?

Similarly, when we come to look at education and the wider society, we are faced with a number of other dilemmas. Should education be regarded as a consumer item (ideal of individual freedom and participation), or as a social service (ideal of social justice)? Is efficiency an appropriate criterion for the operation of an education system? Should education be regarded as socialisation into generally accepted personality characteristics, social norms and values, or should this conception be condemned as stagnant and stultifying and replaced by an unspecifiable individualistic ideal? Should we begin our analysis from the point of view of the system and its goals and needs or from the point of view of the individual and his aims and motives?

Such dilemmas of values and alternative models will always exist.

A changing society inevitably includes contradictory values and an on-going discipline is continually creating and adjusting its models and systems of thought. There are no easy solutions to these fundamental dilemmas. But the first major step is to recognise that the dilemmas exist, that they are fundamentally value conflicts and must be treated as such.

The next step is to try to assess how important the dilemmas are anyway in terms of what actually happens in the educational system. How, and in what form, do educational ideas become influential, if, indeed, they do become influential? It is important to emphasise the interrelationship between ideas and self-interest, between ideas and ideals. Thus, a father's thoughts and actions concerning selection in schools are more likely to be related to factors he perceives in his immediate situation than to any regard for educational theories concerning intelligence or the preserving of knowledge standards. His opinions and actions will be governed more by the success of his own children in the state system and the availability of 'good' schools than by any reference to more basic principles. But, at the same time, attention has to be paid to the system of education and particularly the interrelationship of education and other institutions. Educational plans and policies have to be implemented by individuals who occupy positions in networks of social relationships in organisational settings. Beyond this, organisations themselves exist in particular political, economic and ideational frameworks. In English society during the Middle Ages, the church had the greatest influence over education. In a communist state, today, the central committee of the party or some similar body exerts the greatest power. In most complex societies, however, it is not necessary or possible to locate one single source of power and influence in the education system; there are a number of, often competing, sources of influence.

Certainly, one indirect effect of the influence of the market on the educational system is the necessity that both progressives and idealists find for using advertising techniques to attempt to 'sell' their educational ideas. A part of the process of decision-making and policy implementation in a situation of nation-wide communications is concerned with the mechanics of the process whereby ideals are formulated into slogans for mass consumption and become accepted as general and worthwhile aims. Changes are achieved in democratic societies by the workings of interest groups on public opinion and on the sources of power. Just how influential educational ideas are in this respect is much akin to the way different products compete in the market place for consumers and advocates. Progressives and idealists compete for adherents in the hope that, when there are enough of them, it will be possible to reconstruct schools and society according to their ideas. It is common, therefore, for all groups to employ ideology and to 'manage knowledge' in their hunt for converts. Ideology usually involves a simplification of complex arguments, and educational ideologies include selected or distorted ideas about the educational system, man and society. Emotional outpourings and the manipulation of statistics are used to present ideas which purport to be factual, while also carrying more or less explicit evaluations of the 'facts'. (See, for example, Cox and Dyson, 1969; Rubinstein and Stoneman, 1970; Cuddihy, Gowan and Lindsay, 1970.) Educational ideologies are usually formulated in response to the feeling that some particular element in the prevailing policy is receiving insufficient attention. The neglected element is emphasised and brought to everyone's attention by the selection, intensification and generalisation of certain elements while other elements are neglected. But it often achieves its purpose, which is to convince people of the appropriateness of certain aims. For, by simplifying complex situations, ideologies can help many diverse people to cooperate towards the same goals. Thus, the situation is defined and a particular course of action justified.

It is necessary to try to assess the extent and pervasiveness of advertising techniques and ideologies in education if we are to talk meaningfully about the 'management' of knowledge and education. It is obviously of crucial importance to know whether certain sets of ideas are adopted because of the power or wealth of their promoting groups, or because, for any multitude of reasons, any alternative ideas are refused a hearing or denied an audience. As Geoffrey Esland says (Young, 1971):

> The concept 'public' was elaborated by Blumer to refer to the groups of aggregates who collectively view or use a particular service in society, and, therefore, contribute to public debate about it. Thus, particular orientations in educational practice are located in the ideologies of the dominant publics. It would seem necessary, for example, to consider the Schools Council and educational research bodies in this context; similarly, numerous industrial organisations which hold views on education; various parents' organisations and even the news media. The question one would be asking about these publics is what characterises their thinking about education? How are changing conceptual thresholds for defining valid school experience communicated and made plausible to the teacher and to other publics? How is the dialogue between consumers of education and its professional exponents indicative of changing concepts of order and control?

The rhetorics and ideologies of 'publics' are, of course, located in the socio-cultural processes which support and label particular kinds of enterprise as educationally 'worthwhile'. For example, the subject and pedagogical perspectives of teachers contain 'preferences' which become operative in their explanation of the world and that these are part of the wider historical, educational epistemologies.

How, then, are we to set about the mammoth task of assessing the influence of educational ideas? First, we have to have it constantly in mind that we will need to consider both system and action models. It is important to examine education from the perspective of the goals and motives of individual teachers and pupils, in terms of the aims and needs of education itself and in terms of the functions and purposes it performs for the wider society. Second, we know that the principle of the market is pervasive, both in the sense of imposing efficiency criteria on educational institutions and in requiring educationalists to use advertising techniques to sell their ideas. Third, we are aware that both knowledge and education are 'managed' in such a way as to reinforce certain values whether these be status quo or utopian values. Having clarified this, there are a number of analytical factors which need to be distinguished. It is necessary to look at individuals and their immediate situations, for the action model has indicated how crucial individuals' conceptions of ends and goals and their motivations are for the ultimate realisation of any ideas. Then we must consider the obligations and expectations attached to social positions and roles since the interaction of these with the individual's perceived goals and motives will determine the formulation of certain groups within the wider population which have particular interests or definitions of the situation in common. Interest groups are closely associated with pressure groups which exist to exert their influence on public opinion and on decision makers, and constitute an important part of the decision-making process. Finally, the interrelationship between education and other institutions in society, the economy and the polity, will determine relative priorities and the subservience or otherwise of the educational system, and therefore the likely success of certain educational ideas. The interrelationship between all these factors must be stressed at the outset. Indeed, it will be obvious how difficult it is to distinguish individual and positional definitions of the situation except, perhaps, where the two conflict or are at variance.

It is obviously a platitude to state that the impact of educational ideas on individuals will vary. It is one of the tenets of the sociology of knowledge that the impact will vary according to an individual's social position, in particular his position in the class structure, and this I will come to in a few moments. First, however, it is necessary to examine the notion that reactions are more individual than this, that is, are responses to more immediate situations. Some individuals will be educationalists themselves and their opinions and actions may well result from long consideration of different educational theories and ideas and how well they work in practice. Other individuals (the large majority) are likely to think and react to progressive and idealist educational ideas according to their own or their children's experiences in the educational system (and this is not necessarily related to their social position). Progressive educational ideas appeal to or are condemned by a very broad spectrum of people, some from experience, some from theoretical knowledge, some from entrenched prejudices. It has been asserted, therefore, that an individual's reactions to educational issues cannot be predicted.

This book has been concerned to demonstrate the opposite viewpoint, namely that opinions and attitudes on particular educational issues hang together in such a way as to emphasise the relationship and internal coherence between models and ideas, ideas and structures, in education. It could be hypothesised that the large majority of people have little or no knowledge of educational ideas and that because of this, progressives and idealists resort to the advertiser's techniques of selling and mass communication. Complex ideas are simplified into readily assimilated and adopted aims and goals in attempts to unite largely apathetic consumers. But it might be further hypothesised that such techniques convince and convert nobody. Individuals will simply select and sort the predigested ideas and slogans in order to reinforce already existing attitudes and convictions.

However, to state that educational ideas and attitudes can be inferred from opinions concerning structure and organisation, and that all these are related to a particular social and political philosophy, is a rather different assertion from that which states that an individual's (educational) ideas can be related to his social position. The sociology of knowledge is concerned with the social location of ideas. It shows how the individual's ideas and opinions are derived in much the same way as he derives his social roles, and that particular ideas are associated with particular positions. We must examine this suggestion, therefore, that individuals in certain positions react in predictable ways such that it might be possible to group them and generalise about their responses to certain educational ideas.

Teachers provide an interesting example here. They are in a

crucial position as the medium through which educational ideas are converted into actions. Do teachers respond in any predictable way to any set of educational ideas? It can be hypothesised that a college-trained teacher will be more responsive to progressive ideas than a university graduate; an older teacher is likely to be more critical of new educational notions than a young teacher fresh from college. Teachers are currently at work in particular kinds of educational institutions and their reactions are likely to be at least partly a result of this. Thus, teachers in a junior school are more likely to be receptive to progressive ideas than teachers in a grammar school; teachers in universities are likely to be more idealistic than teachers in a technical college. But the opinions and attitudes of those in powerful positions must be considered too, since an idealistic junior school headmaster can exert considerable pressure on the teachers in his school. We know there is great diversity in this respect since many teachers experience role conflict if their individual convictions do not square with the requirements and expectations of their particular position.

Where a number of teachers feel particularly strongly about any educational idea, they can come together in interest groups and pressure groups designed to promote that idea. The teachers' professional organisations (National Union of Teachers, National Association of Schoolmasters, etc.) have not been particularly influential in promoting particular educational ideas because the profession itself is so divided over these issues. Resolutions have been passed by teaching organisations. Thus, for example, the NUT passed a resolution in favour of comprehensive secondary schooling at its annual conference in 1969. This resolution called on the government 'to make the necessary legislative changes to bring about comprehensive education by abolishing selection for secondary education' (*Teacher*, 18 April 1969). In general, the NUT can be expected to be more sympathetic to progressive ideas than the NAS and the other professional organisations. This is because membership of the NUT is predominantly younger, college-trained teachers based in junior and secondary modern schools. The NAS is more concerned to establish a career structure for teachers and to stress the professional elements of teaching. University graduates in selective secondary schools make up the bulk of membership of the other professional organisations.

Teachers as a whole are as divided over educational ideas as the population in general, although it is possible to hypothesise that certain groups within the profession will be more sympathetic to progressive ideas and other groups to idealist ideas. A number of pressure groups have developed within the teaching profession designed to promote specific educational goals. The Council for

Educational Advance is an umbrella organisation which was successful in making education an important issue in the 1964 general election, and also fought the cuts in educational spending in 1968. STOPP is an organisation with the express aim of banning corporal punishment from schools and advocating a less authoritarian structure with pupil councils, and with teachers and students allowed a share in the running of the school. A number of ginger groups have sprung up within the NUT such as 'Rank and File', or within the profession such as the Society for the Promotion of Educational Reform through Teacher Training (SPERTT). A recent example of the formation of an idealist pressure group was marked by the publication of the so-called *Black Papers*. These consisted of collections of articles by teachers and others designed to publicise the idealist conception of education in the face of what they saw as the progressive threat.

The formation of such pressure groups is usually conceived on a nation-wide basis, but their real influence is mostly on a smaller scale. This is usually related to the extent to which their sympathisers become members of decision-making bodies or committees making policy recommendations, or are in powerful positions such as headships or chairmen of governing bodies. Teachers themselves are in a unique position of power as a result of their autonomy in the classroom. They can determine to what extent policy decisions are implemented. Because of the importance of the teacher's opinions, it is to the teachers themselves that progressives and idealists must make their appeal. Although in many cases a teacher's attitudes and convictions will be formed early (as a result of his own experiences and background), nevertheless his teacher-training will mark his first introduction to purely educational philosophies and practices. Thus, it can be suggested that the educational ideals of those who teach our teachers are of central importance in determining what goes on in all our educational establishments. For many years the university ideal held sway over the education process. The universities defined the goals of the education process and dictated the means whereby these goals were to be achieved. The teacher-training colleges were very much the poor relations in the higher education system. Their purpose was unclear. On the one hand, they tried to copy the university ideal of a continuing general education, a striving after the knowledge-ideal. On the other hand, they had to be concerned with more mundane matters of practical teaching. The popularity of progressive educational ideas occurred mainly in the colleges of education and hence most of their influence has been in infant and junior schools where, for the most part, college of education trained teachers teach. University graduate schools of education have for longer remained attached to the idealist conception of education. Thus, our grammar schools have also retained their idealist conceptions, partly because they wish to be associated with the universities anyway, but partly also because grammar school teachers are primarily university products themselves.

The universities, as a collective and as separate institutions, can be considered as a powerful pressure group for the upholding of the knowledge-ideal and other idealist conceptions of education. Despite increasing financial dependence, the universities have been able to maintain their position as leaders in the educational system. The universities influence the secondary school curriculum because of their own entrance requirements and the part they play in GCE assessment. They are concerned with the training of teachers through their institutes and departments of education. The conception of the education process advocated by the universities is an important factor in determining what goes on in all our educational establishments at all levels.

The importance of the universities goes further than their influence as a collective, however. A university position gives authority and weight to any individual stating his own ideas. Thus, most unorthodox educational thinkers will nevertheless wish to see their doctrines and ideas discussed there. In terms of the individuals within universities, there is a great deal of disagreement concerning educational theories and ideas, as would be expected. But this does not detract from the fact that universities give power, status and respect to their position holders which enables them to speak with authority and to gain an audience which might be denied to someone in a lesser position. Thus, university teachers and researchers are coopted or elected on to decision-making committees or boards or are asked to give evidence and their position guarantees them a hearing. Progressives and idealists must make their mark on our universities if they are to be influential in the educational system.

Another social position that is supposed to give scope for generalisation is that of 'parent'. Is it possible to classify parents in order to be able to generalise about their attitudes to educational ideas? It can be suggested that certain parents have interests in common as a result of their being similarly placed with regard to the educational system. Professional parents with children at public schools are likely to be highly sympathetic to the view that education should be organised according to market principles. They are more likely to be in favour of the idealist conception of the education process, not necessarily because they value the knowledge-ideal (although this may be the case), but because they perceive the value of such an education in terms of the advantages it gives for access to universities and/or high status occupations. Similarly, many middle-class and working-class parents, whose children have been successful in the state system, are likely to endorse the selective system partly because of the perceived advantages that grammar school and university education will give their children, and partly because of a respect for the mystique of the idealist conception of education as it is maintained by such institutions. Progressive ideals and demands for educational changes will meet with little sympathy from such groups. Only if parents feel their children are at a disadvantage or are in a relatively deprived (see Chapter 1) position will they listen with interest to criticisms of the present structure and to proposed alternatives. Of particular importance in this respect are the middle-class parents and status dissenting working class parents whose children have not been particularly successful in the state system. Such groups are likely to be more vocal in their protestations than the large body of status assenting working-class parents where the tendency is to accept the decisions of those in authority with a fatalistic resignation and to look with general disfavour on any proposed changes to the system.

It is largely as a result of progressive ideas on education that attempts are being made to involve parents more directly in the work of the schools. For many interested parents such pressures are largely irrelevant because they are already involved and concerned. It is on the large body of parents to whom education remains a mystery (or a necessary evil) that such attempts are focused. Such moves are partly a result of findings that children whose parents are interested and involved achieve better results, and partly they arise from a view of education as individual development arising primarily from experiences of all kinds and therefore requiring the breakdown of barriers between education and the world outside. Such parental involvement is obviously not required by the idealist who sees his job as the preservation of the knowledge-ideal. Indeed involving parents, with their utilitarian conceptions of the education process, may be positively harmful in removing and destroying the mystique of the scholarship ideal. But even for many progressives, attempts to involve parents are at variance with attempts to 'professionalise' teaching by establishing teaching techniques on educational and psychological learning theories. Thus, 'discovery methods', 'the new maths', the Initial Teaching Alphabet (ITA) are likely to alienate large bodies of parents and work against their active involvement.

For the most part, parents are remote from debates concerning the intellectual nature of man and educational standards. Parents are often confused by notions of elitism and egalitarianism even though certain platitudes may strike a note of harmony or discord. A number of national organisations of parents do exist, often with extensive local branches which are intended to mobilise parental support for a number of educational ideas. The Comprehensive Schools Committee, under the chairmanship of Michael Armstrong, is a non-party organisation for the advancement of comprehensive secondary education. The Confederation for the Advancement of State Education (CASE) is a national organisation with active local branches designed to promote increased investment in state education. The Advisory Centre for Education (ACE) was founded in 1960, 'one of the earlier signs that the new decade would be concerned with parents, home–school relationships and pupils' motivation'. The Home and School Council was designed to promote increased home and school contact.

Parents are potentially a most important source of pressure over what goes on in education. But the precise influence of educational ideas on parents is probably very small. Parents have not constituted an effective pressure group at national level, probably because they feel they cannot influence the central government. However, at the local level, parental involvement has been more successful over certain issues that have caught the public imagination. The way education is administered in the USA shows how important parents can be in the running of the education system. In this country, parents who feel their interests are not being met, either in general or on a particular issue can form pressure groups to further their goals. Likewise, individual parents can exert their influence by becoming members of local government bodies in order to attempt to divert attention accordingly.

The issue of comprehensive education provides an example of an instance where local groups of parents frequently became involved (see examples quoted by Batley et al., 1970; Benn and Simon, 1970). Committees were formed to fight for comprehensive plans to be adopted by local education committees and, in retaliation, defence societies and 'save our schools' committees were formed around individual grammar schools. Petitions were signed and in some areas protest meetings and marches were held. But even here the influence of educational theories as such was restricted to small numbers of dedicated individuals fighting to promote particular educational ideas. Parents were influenced more by the slogans employed by different pressure groups: 'the waste of ability' and 'equal educational opportunity' on the one hand, 'the destruction of our grammar schools' and 'the decline in standards' on the other.

From parents and parental pressure groups it is necessary to consider public opinion in general, as a force in the educational system. Educational ideas seldom affect public opinion directly, only when they have been filtered and incorporated into an existing body of social and political ideology. The ideas themselves have to be transformed for mass consumption, and climates of opinion seem to result more from successful advertising techniques than from reasoned arguments.

Lester Smith (1957) has suggested a simple 'swing of the pendulum' theory to explain why climates of opinion alter, values shift and changes in structure are demanded. In other words, after a period of time, people simply get fed up with the education system much in the way that they do with politicians, and public opinion moves in favour of giving the other side a chance. However, it surely needs more than this to explain why, at the end of the Second World War, the general climate of opinion was in favour of a large extension of educational opportunities. The new position was based largely on principles of increasing social justice and equality and, to further this, there was a willingness to hand over to central governments greater control and direction of educational affairs. Neither does such a swing theory explain why, with the increasing affluence of the 1950s and 1960s, these ideals declined in public favour to be replaced by market criteria of choice and efficiency. For the most part, the general public cannot and do not wish to follow the details of educational disputes. But public opinion is always related to dominant (usually long-lasting rather than transitory) values. Thus, public opinion usually desires stability. For this reason, educational ideas which include widespread change are likely to be ignored or deplored by public opinion unless and until value changes have been accepted first. In other words, people have to be convinced that the new way will be worth all the disruption and lack of predictability because it will be working towards something really worthwhile. For the most part, people are not convinced that the structural changes and changes in pedagogy proposed by many progressives in education will do this.

Politics and education

The often heard plea that education should be 'taken out of politics' is to misunderstand the nature of both activities: education is political through and through. The situation is highly complex, however, not least because of the wide variety of influences which are brought to bear upon the development of educational policy such as the Department of Education Science, political party ideologies, pressure groups, local educa authorities, the schools and professional and parental associations. Through all these, educational ideas are filtered, digested and reproduced in an acceptable form for mass consumption.

Education is not only a means to individual development, it is also the instrument for the creation of a better society. The structure of education has a profound effect on the social structure. For this reason it cannot be divorced from politics. Politics is about the competition for power by organised groups. If these groups disagree strongly about education then education is made a political issue. The oversimplified alternatives usually proposed are an education system which cultivates an intellectual elite or an education system that provides a general education shared by all which would form the basis for a greater sense of community. Both educational theories are first and foremost political and social theories centring on opposing attitudes to elites.

The role of central government in the present situation of local autonomy and national and local pressure groups is largely one of compromise. It is extremely doubtful whether a change of government, bringing to power political groups with different policies emerging from different philosophies, would produce a fundamental transformation. The facts of administration and the division of responsibilities between central and local government frequently override changes in political philosophies and provide for 'stability' or 'stagnation', according to one's own views. The importance of party politics in educational decisions, therefore, is to act as a force precipitating changes, where the central government's role is to re-establish a temporary equilibrium.

The direction such equilibrium positions take depends on temporary or more permanent power balances and compromise agreements. One way of looking at these 'equilibrium positions' is as ideologies of the ruling class. However, there is sufficient real party conflict in British politics for us to reject this as oversimplified. Any actual situation in education represents a compromise position between conflicting interests. Such definitions are the end product of a bargaining process which may or may not mean an agreed definition of the situation. If there is no agreement, the compromise situation will be broken with a change of political power.

The compromise model includes the possibility that change may be generated within the education system itself, if there is ever sufficient unity over or a powerful enough majority advocating a particular educational change. Thus, change may be generated within the system itself by autonomous development, or as a result of an alteration in power within or outside the system, or as a result of a change in the values governing the use of power within or outside the system. Change occurs, therefore, when different ideas are brought to bear on a situation and a redefinition is made. The redefinition will finally result in a new compromise, depending on the new balance of power, either political or within the institution itself.

It seems, however, that major decisions concerning educational development will not be made in accordance with the rubrics of professional educationalists because educationalists themselves are so utterly divided as to their goals and values. When the philosophy behind a system is not very explicitly formulated apart from a few vague (and often contradictory) generalisations, as in education at present, decisions will be formulated in response to a balance of economic and political pressures. Thus, in terms of actual policy decisions, the educational ideas themselves are not so important as the compromise political and economic positions that are most common, and the 'contradictory' principles which, nevertheless, form the basis for practical solutions. This does not mean that educational ideas themselves are unimportant in shaping the course of events. It does mean that the outcome of educational ideas is commonly very different from what those who had the ideas in the first place planned or hoped. This is primarily because of the complex interrelationship between ideas and structures, between ideas and ideals. Our interest began with educational ideas. It developed from this to concepts, structures and to socio-political ideals. This is because the relation between ideas and policies and practices is never direct. It is always mediated by particular interpretations and by alternative interpretations. The role of moral evaluation, of social and political ideology is, therefore, crucial.

Suggestions for further reading

General

HIRST, P. H. and PETERS, R. S. (1970), *The Logic of Education*, London: Routledge & Kegan Paul. A critical assessment of 'progressive' and 'idealist' philosophies of education.

WEAVER, T. R. (1970), *Unity and Diversity in Education*, DES Educational Information Pamphlet. An appraisal of the pedagogical implications of 'progressive' and 'idealist' approaches to education.

Intelligence

BUTCHER, H. J. and LOMAX, D. E. (1972), *Readings in Human Intelligence*, London: Methuen. A collection of readings describing new advances in the area of intelligence theory and measurement.

VERNON, P. E. (1969), *Intelligence and Cultural Environment*, London: Methuen. A consideration of the influence of environmental factors on intelligence.

WATSON, P. (1970), 'The new IQ test', *New Society*, 22 January. A discussion of the difficulties of constructing IQ tests and a description of a new test designed to overcome some of the difficulties.

The knowledge-ideal

COX, C. B. and DYSON, A. E. (eds) (1969), *Black Papers* I, II and III, Critical Quarterly Society. Collections of articles justifying idealist education and criticising present educational structures and proposed changes.

ELIOT, T. S. (1968), *Notes Towards the Definition of Culture*, London: Faber. A justification of the existence of an elite culture; its significance and worth.

OAKESHOTT, M. (1962), *Rationalism in Politics*, London: Methuen. A statement of the distinction between practical and technical knowledge and criticism of contemporary education for its neglect of practical knowledge.

WILSON, BRYAN (1970), *The Youth Culture and the Universities*, London: Faber. A description of the antagonism between contemporary student culture and the university ideal.

Equal educational opportunity

ADAM, RUTH (1969), 'Project Headstart: LBJ's one success?', *New Society*, 30 October.
CORBETT, ANNE (1969), 'Are educational priority areas working?', *New Society*, 13 November. These articles assess projects in America and Britain to counter educational deprivation.
KELSALL, R. K. and H. M. (1971), *Social Disadvantage and Educational Opportunity*, New York: Holt, Rinehart & Winston. Comprehensive review of the problem of educational deprivation and compensatory experimental schemes.

Selection in education

BARKER-LUNN, JOAN (1970), *Streaming in the Primary School*, NFER. A detailed operational study of streaming in this country.
DAVIES, H. (1965), *Culture and the Grammar School*, University of Nottingham Institute of Education. The contribution that grammar schools have to make and a plea for their continued existence.
GOLDBERG, M. L., PASSOW, A. H. and JUSTMAN, J. (1966), *The Effects of Ability Grouping*, Columbia: Teachers' College Press. The most comprehensive experimental study yet carried out in this field.
VERNON, P. E. (ed.) (1957), *Secondary School Selection*, London: Methuen. These books review the problems associated with selection for secondary education and summarise the results of a considerable amount of relevant research.
YATES, A. and PIDGEON, D. A. (1957), *Admission to Grammar Schools*, London: Newnes.

Education and society

HALSEY, A. H., FLOUD, J. and ANDERSON, C. A. (eds) (1961), *Education, Economy and Society*, New York: Free Press.
MUSGRAVE, P. W. (ed.) (1970), *Sociology, History and Education*, London: Methuen. These books are collections of articles showing the interrelationship of education and other variables.
YOUNG, M. F. D. (ed.) (1971), *Knowledge and Control*, London: Collier-Macmillan. These articles discuss definitions of knowledge and the connection between education and social order.

Bibliography

ACTON, H. B. (1971), *The Morals of Markets*, London: Longman.

ADAM, RUTH (1969), 'Project Headstart: LBJ's one success?', *New Society*, 30 October.

ARMITAGE, P., SMITH, C. and ALPER, P. (1970), *Decision Models for Educational Planning*, London: Allen Lane, The Penguin Press.

BANKS, O. (1955), *Parity and Prestige in English Secondary Education*, London: Routledge & Kegan Paul.

BANKS, O. (1968), *The Sociology of Education*, London: Batsford.

BANTOCK, G. H. (1963), *Education in an Industrial Society*, London: Faber.

BARKER-LUNN, JOAN (1970), *Streaming in the Primary School*, National Foundation for Educational Research.

BARRY, B. (1965), *Political Argument*, London: Routledge & Kegan Paul.

BATLEY, R. *et al.* (1970), *Going Comprehensive*, London: Routledge & Kegan Paul.

BENN, C. and SIMON, B. (1970), *Half Way There*, New York: McGraw-Hill.

BERGER, P. and LUCKMAN, T. (1967), *The Social Construction of Reality*, London: Allen Lane, The Penguin Press.

BERNSTEIN, B. (1970a), 'The open school', *Where*, Supplement 12, March.

BERNSTEIN, B. (1970b), 'Education and Society', *New Society*, 26 February.

BLAUG, M. (1970), *An Introduction to the Economics of Education*, London: Allen Lane, The Penguin Press.

BOWLES, FRANK (1963), *Access to Higher Education*, UNESCO.

CANNON, C. (1964), 'Some variations on the teacher's role', *Education for Teaching*, 64, May.

CARLSSON, GOSTA (1958), *Social Mobility and the Class Structure*, Lund, Sweden: Gleerup.

CARTER, M. (1962), *Home, School and Work*, Oxford: Pergamon Press.

CARTWRIGHT, D. and ZANDER, A. (eds) (1953), *Group Dynamics*, London: Tavistock.

CENTERS, R. (1949), in *American Sociological Review*, February.

CLARKE, F. (1940), *Education and Social Change*, London: Sheldon Press.

COHEN, P. (1968), *Modern Social Theory*, London: Heinemann Educational Books.

CORBETT, ANNE (1969), 'Are educational priority areas working', *New Society*, 13 November.

COSER, L. (1965), *The Functions of Social Conflict*, London: Routledge & Kegan Paul.

COX, C. B. and DYSON, A. E. (eds) (1969), *Black Papers I, II and III*, Critical Quarterly Society.

CUDDIHY, R., GOWAN, D. and LINDSAY, C. (1970), *The Red Paper*, Edinburgh: Islander Publications.

DAVIES, IOAN (1970), 'The management of knowledge', *Sociology*, 4:1, January.

DAVIS, KINGSLEY (1948), *Human Society*, New York: Macmillan Co.

DAVIS, R. (1967), *The Grammar School*, Harmondsworth: Penguin.

DAWE, A. (1970), 'The two sociologies', *British Journal of Sociology*, XXI:2.

DEWEY, F. (1916), *Democracy and Education*, New York: Macmillan Co.

DEWEY, F. (1938), *Experience and Education*, New York: Macmillan Co.

DOUGLAS, J. W. B. (1964), *The Home and the School*, London: MacGibbon & Kee.

DOUGLAS, J. W. B. (1968), *All Our Future*, London: Peter Davies.

DURKHEIM, E. (1956), *Education and Society*, Chicago: Free Press.

EGGLESTON, S. J. (1967), *The Social Context of the School*, London: Routledge & Kegan Paul.

EKSTROM, R. B. (1959), *Experimental Studies of Homogeneous Grouping: A Review of the Literature*, Princeton, New Jersey: Educational Testing Service.

ELIOT, T. S. (1968), *Notes Towards the Definition of Culture*, London: Faber.

ETZIONI, A. (1961), *A Comparative Analysis of Complex Organisations*, New York: Free Press.

ETZIONI, A. (1964), *Modern Organisations*, New York: Basic Books.

EYSENCK, H. J. (1971), *Race, Intelligence and Education*, London: Temple Smith.

FLOUD, JEAN and HALSEY, A. (1958), 'The sociology of education: a trend report and bibliography', *Current Sociology* 7 (3).

FLOUD, JEAN (1962), 'Teaching in the affluent society', *British Journal of Sociology*, December.

FORD, JULIENNE (1969), *Social Class and the Comprehensive School*, London: Routledge & Kegan Paul.

FOSTER, P. (1965), *Education and Social Change in Ghana*, London: Routledge & Kegan Paul.

GLASS, D. (1954), *Social Mobility in Britain*, London: Routledge & Kegan Paul.

GOFFMAN, E. (1959), *The Presentation of Self in Everyday Life*, New York: Anchor Books.

GOLDBERG, M. (1966), *The Effects of Ability Grouping*, Columbia: Teachers' College Press.

GUILFORD, J. P. (1965), 'An analysis of education', in *New Education*, September.

GUILFORD, J. P. (1967), *The Nature of Human Intelligence*, New York: McGraw-Hill.

HALSEY, A. H. (ed.) (1961), *Ability and Educational Opportunity*, OECD.

HALSEY, A. H., FLOUD, J. and ANDERSON, C. A. (1961), *Education, Economy and Society*, New York: Free Press.

HANS, NICHOLAS (1949), *Comparative Education*, London: Routledge & Kegan Paul.

HARGREAVES, D. H. (1967), *Social Relations in a Secondary School*, London: Routledge & Kegan Paul.

HARRIS, R. and SELDON, A. (1963, 1965, 1970), Reports, *Choice in Welfare*, London: Institute of Economic Affairs.

HIMMELWEIT, H., *et al.* (1952), 'The views of adolescents on some aspects of the social class structure', *British Journal of Sociology*, June.

HIRST, P. H. and PETERS, R. S. (1970), *The Logic of Education*, London: Routledge & Kegan Paul.

HOLT, JOHN (1970a), *How Children Learn*, Harmondsworth: Penguin.

HOLT, JOHN (1970b), *How Children Fail*, Harmondsworth, Penguin.

HOPPER, E. I. (1968), 'A typology for the classification of educational systems', *Sociology*, 2:1.

HOYLE, E. (1969), *The Role of the Teacher*, London: Routledge & Kegan Paul.

HUDSON, L. (1966), *Contrary Imaginations*, London: Methuen.

JACKSON, B. (1964), *Streaming: An Educational System in Miniature*, London: Routledge & Kegan Paul.

JACKSON, B. and MCALHONE, B. (eds) (1969), *Verdict on the Facts*, ACE.

JAHODA, P. (1952), 'Job attitudes and job choice among secondary modern school leavers', in *Occupational Psychology*, April and October.

JENSEN, ARTHUR (1969), 'How much can we boost IQ and scholastic attainment?', *Harvard Educational Review*, 39:1, Winter.

JINKS, P. C. (1964), 'An investigation into the date of birth on subsequent school performance', *Educational Research*, VI:3.

KING, R. (1969), *Values and Involvement in a Grammar School*, London: Routledge & Kegan Paul.

KLEIN, J. (1965), *Samples from English Cultures*, London: Routledge & Kegan Paul.

KOGAN, MAURICE (1971), *The Politics of Education*, Harmondsworth: Penguin.

KUMAR, KRISHNAN (1969), 'Excellence and anarchy', *Listener*, 16 October.

LAUWERYS, J. A. (ed.) (1968), *Ideals and Ideologies*, London: Evans.

LAUWERYS, J. A. (ed.) (1969), *Education and the Economy*, London: Evans.

LAYARD, R., MOSER, C. and KING, J. (1969), *The Impact of Robbins*, Harmondsworth: Penguin.

LEAVIS, F. R. (1948), 'Mass civilisation and minority culture' in *Education and the University*, London: Chatto & Windus.

LEAVIS, F. R. (1969), 'English—unrest and continuity', *The Times Literary Supplement*, 29 May, No. 3509.

LESTER SMITH, W. O. (1957), *Education*, Harmondsworth: Penguin.

LESTER SMITH, W. O. (1966), *The Government of Education*, Harmondsworth: Penguin.

LOCKE, JOHN (1934), *Some Thoughts Concerning Education*, ed. by R. H. Quick, New York: Cambridge University Press.

MACHLUP, F. (1970), *Education and Economic Growth*, University of Nebraska Press.

MAIZELS, JOAN (1970), 'How school-leavers rate teachers', *New Society*, 24 September.

MANN, HORACE (1850), *Lectures on Education*, London: Arno.

MANNHEIM, KARL (1936), *Ideology and Utopia*, London: Routledge & Kegan Paul.

MANNHEIM, KARL (1957), *Freedom, Power and Democratic Planning*, London: Routledge & Kegan Paul.

MAXWELL, J. (1961), *The Level and Trend of National Intelligence*, Council for Research in Education No. 66, London University Press.

MAYS, J. B. (1962), *Education and the Urban Child*, Liverpool University Press.

MCINTOSH, D. M. (1959), *Educational Guidance and the Pool of Ability*, University of London Press.

MERTON, R. K. (1957), *Social Theory and Social Structure*, Chicago: Free Press

MORRISH, I. (1972), *The Sociology of Education*, London: Allen & Unwin.

MUSGRAVE, P. W. (1965), *The Sociology of Education*, London: Methuen.

MUSGRAVE, P. W. (1968), *The School as an Organisation*, London: Macmillan.

MUSGRAVE, P. W. (1970), *Sociology, History and Education*, London: Methuen.

MUSGROVE, F. and TAYLOR, P. H. (1969), *Society and the Teacher's Role*, London: Routledge & Kegan Paul.

NEWSON, J. and E. (1963), *Patterns of Infant Care*, London: Allen & Unwin.

OAKESHOTT, M. (1962), *Rationalism in Politics*, London: Methuen.

PARKHURST, HELEN (1922), *Education on the Dalton Plan*, London: Bell.

PARSONS, T. (1951), *The Social System*, Chicago: Free Press.

PEDLEY, R. (1963), *The Comprehensive School*, Harmondsworth: Pelican.

PETERSON, A. D. C. (1952), *A Hundred Years of Education*, London: Duckworth.

PIAGET, J. (1926), *The Language and Thought of the Child*, London: Routledge.

PIAGET, J. (1932), *The Moral Judgment of the Child*, London: Routledge.

Plowden Report (1967), London: HMSO.

REEVES, M. (1966), *Eighteen Plus*, London: Faber.

REX, JOHN (1961), *Key Problems in Sociological Theory*, London: Routledge & Kegan Paul.

RICE, A. K. (1970), *The Modern University: A Model Organisation*, London: Tavistock.

Robbins Report (1963), London: HMSO.

ROSENTHAL, R. and JACOBSON, L. (1968), *Pygmalion in the Classroom*, New York: Rinehart & Winston.

ROSZAK, T. (1970), *The Making of a Counter Culture*, London: Faber.

ROUSSEAU, J.-J. (1961), *Émile*, London: Dent, Everyman's Library.

RUBINSTEIN, D. and STONEMAN, C. (eds) (1970), *Education for Democracy*, Harmondsworth: Penguin.

RUNCIMAN, W. G. (1966), *Relative Deprivation and Social Justice*, London: Routledge & Kegan Paul.

SILVERMAN, D. (1968), 'Formal organisations or industrial sociology: towards a social action analysis of organisations', *Sociology*, 2:2, May.

SILVERMAN, D. (1971), *Theory of Organisations*, London: Heinemann.

SMITH, MARSHALL and BISSELL, JOAN (1970), 'The impact of Headstart: the Westinghouse Ohio Headstart evaluation', in *Harvard Educational Review*, March.

STOTT, D. H. and LEWIS, D. G. (1966), in *British Journal of Psychology*, November.

SUGARMAN, B. (1970), 'Classroom friends and leaders', *New Society*, 22 January.

SUTTON, P. (1967), 'Correlation between streaming and season of birth in secondary schools', *British Journal of Educational Psychology*, 37.

SWIFT, D. F. (1969), *The Sociology of Education*, London: Routledge & Kegan Paul.

TAYLOR, GEORGE (1971), 'North and south: the educational split', *New Society*, 4 March.

TITMUSS, R. (1971), *The Gift of Relationship*, London: Allen & Unwin.

TURNER, R. (1960), 'Sponsored and contest mobility', *American Sociological Review*.

VAIZEY, J. (1958), *The Costs of Education*, London: Allen & Unwin.

VAIZEY, J. and ROBINSON, E. A. G. (1966), *The Economics of Education*, London: Macmillan.

VAIZEY, J. and SHEEHAN, A. (1968), *Resources for Education*, London: Allen & Unwin.

VERNON, P. E. (1968), 'What is potential ability?', in the *Bulletin of the British Psychology Society*, October.

VERNON, P. E. (1969), *Intelligence and Cultural Environment*, London: Methuen.

WARNOCK, MARY (1970), 'The stigma of school-teaching', *New Society*, 8 January.

WATSON, PETER (1970), 'The new IQ test', *New Society*, 22 January.

WEAVER, T. R. (1970), *Unity and Diversity in Education*, DES Educational Information Pamphlet.

WEBER, M. (1947), *The Theory of Social and Economic Organisation*, London: Oxford University Press.

WEST, E. G. (1965), *Education and the State*, Institute of Economic Affairs.

WEST, E. G. (1967), *Education: A Framework for Choice*, Institute of Economic Affairs.

WEST, E. G. (1968), *Economics, Education and the Politicians*, Institute of Economic Affairs.

WILLIAMS, RAYMOND (1961a), *Culture and Society*, Harmondsworth: Penguin.

WILLIAMS, RAYMOND (1961b), *The Long Revolution*, London: Chatto & Windus.

WILSON, BRYAN (1963), 'The teacher's role—a sociological analysis', *British Journal of Sociology*, June.

WILSON, BRYAN (1970), *The Youth Culture and the Universities*, London: Faber.

YATES, A. (ed.) (1966), *Grouping in Education*, UNESCO, Institute for Education, New York: Wiley.

YATES, A. and PIDGEON, D. A. (1959-60), 'The effects of streaming', in *Educational Research*, 2.

YOUNG, DOUGLAS and BRANDIS, WALTER (1967), 'Two types of streaming and their probable application in comprehensive schools', *Bulletin*, University of London Institute of Education, XL.

YOUNG, M. (1958), *The Rise of the Meritocracy*, London: Thames & Hudson.

YOUNG, M. F. D. (1971), *Knowledge and Control*, London: Collier-Macmillan.

ZNANIECKI, F. (1940), *The Social Role of the Man of Knowledge*, Columbia University Press.

Index